AF316689

Cyber Resilience

A Strategic Handbook for Business Leaders

By

Rohit Srivastwa & Aalok Karnik

Made with ❤ on the Notion Press Platform
www.notionpress.com

You know how it is. You pick up a book, flip to the dedication, and find that, once again, the author has dedicated a book to someone else and not to you.

Not this time.

We may know each other well OR just been an online acquaintance
We may have met recently OR we haven't seen each other for long

Despite all, **This one's for you.**

Wish you the best for building a secure business

Foreword - 1

Cybersecurity is the bedrock of trust in our interconnected world, indeed it's about safeguarding our way of life. As our reliance on digital technology is growing exponentially, cybersecurity is becoming a critical component of national security and economic stability. It is particularly important for business leaders to understand the inherent cyber security risks.

"Cyber Resilience: A Strategic Handbook for Business Leaders" is a timely guide, crafted to bridge the knowledge gap between technical experts and decision-makers. Cybersecurity is no longer a domain confined to IT departments but a critical business requirement demanding strategic oversight by business leaders.

Through real-world examples and actionable advice, it empowers leaders via insight into best practices, regulatory requirements, and emerging trends. This will help them to make informed decisions safeguarding their organizations' digital assets. It also underscores the importance of fostering a culture of security awareness, where every employee plays a role in defending against cyber adversaries.

I strongly believe that this handbook by Rohit & Aalok will serve as an invaluable resource for business leaders, enabling them to strategize a robust cyber defence program for their organizations making them resilient in the face of cyber-threats.

Padma Vibhushan Dr. Raghunath Mashelkar is a renowned scientist and former Director General of the Council of Scientific and Industrial Research (CSIR)

Foreword - 2

Cyber Security is one of the major risks for individuals and business and social organisations in these complex times for the world. With geo-political tensions simmering and many countries having daggers drawn, physically and metaphorically against others, complacency is not an option.

With the clouds of a cyber-attack always looming, there is need for a strategic response. Organisations must move beyond just appointing a CISO and investing in End Point Security to investing in comprehensive preventive, predictive and proactive processes to build true resilience.

This book by Rohit & Aalok is timely and comprehensive. It provides a playbook for the CEO, the CISO, and the business leader of any corporation. It also provides many nuggets of wisdom for individuals who are interested in this area and Governments who seek to protect their countries, corporations, and citizens from cyber terrorism.

I recommend this book to all intelligent practitioners and knowledge seekers.

Dr. Ganesh Natarajan is Chairman of Honeywell, GTT Solutions and Lighthouse Communities and an expert on digital success.

Table of Contents

Chapter 1

Nobody is going to attack us

Remember criminals do not discriminate, and if you are vulnerable, you WILL BE attacked.

Above reasons are ample motivation for an attacker to plan, orchestrate, and execute an attack against you.

1. Let's look at a few real-world attacks.

A surge in sophisticated cyber-attacks have left organizations reeling from the devastating consequences. From massive data breaches to disruptive ransomware attacks, a rapidly evolving threat landscape, underscores the urgent need for robust cybersecurity measures.

DELL 49 million customer data breach (2024)

Year	2024, USA
Entity	Dell Technologies
Business	Computing giant well known for servers, endpoint computing and services
Attacker	Investigation still ongoing as the date of publishing this book. Not attributed yet
Impact	<ul><li>Information of approximately 49 million customers</li><li>Name, Physical address, order information, , date of order, etc</li></ul>
Read More	https://www.bleepingcomputer.com/news/security/dell-warns-of-data-breach-49-million-customers-allegedly-affected/

NIC Email System Compromise (2021)

Year	2021, India
Entity	National Informatics Center (NIC)
Business	Provide email services to government officials
Attacker	Attributed to state sponsored threat actor
Impact	Allegedly: • Indian Government email accounts were targeted • Sensitive information was stolen
Read More	https://www.thehindu.com/news/national/data-breaches-expose-emails-passwords-of-several-government-officials-to-hackers/article60676924.ece

JBS Foods Ransomware Attack (2021)

Year	2021, USA
Entity	JBS Foods
Business	Large meat processing company
Attacker	REvil ransomware group
Impact	<ul><li>Ransomware attack across USA and Australia</li><li>Temporary shutdown of JBS critical infrastructure</li><li>JBS forced to cease operations at 13 US meat processing plants</li></ul>
Read More	https://en.wikipedia.org/wiki/JBS_S.A._ransomware_attack

Cognizant Ransomware Attack (2020)

Year	2020, India
Entity	Cognizant, India
Business	Multinational IT services company
Attacker	Maze ransomware group
Impact	<ul><li>Ransomware attack disrupted operations and affected client services</li><li>Corporate endpoints were encrypted</li><li>Attack resulted in data theft and significant financial losses.</li></ul>
Read More	https://techcrunch.com/2020/04/18/cognizant-maze-ransomware/

SolarWinds Supply Chain Attack (2020)

Year	2020, USA
Entity	SolarWinds, USA
Business	Leading provider of network management software
Attacker	Alleged but unconfirmed - Russian Foreign Intelligence Service
Impact	• Attackers inserted malicious code into SolarWinds software updates • Sophisticated Supply Chain Attack on the software update distribution mechanism • Unauthorized access to 1000s of SolarWinds client's networks • Data exfiltrated over an extended period.
Read More	https://www.techtarget.com/whatis/feature/SolarWinds-hack-explained-Everything-you-need-to-know

Similar attack happened recently on similar platforms like Kaseya. Similarly, Log4j crisis could have been a supply chain fiasco. Alert network defenders actively thwarted majority of the attacks in a timely manner.

Kudankulam nuclear power plant data breach (2019)

Year	2019, India
Entity	Kudankulam nuclear power plant, India
Business	Provide critical services (electricity) to nation.
Attacker	Lazarus group from North Korea created a purpose built Dtrack malware which collected information from the plant's IT network.
Impact	• Admin credentials were stolen and leveraged to deepen access into the environment. • Malware detected by CERT-India after detection of an infected PC with access to administrative network. Only IT environment was affected not the actual OT environment of the nuclear power plant
Read More	https://economictimes.indiatimes.com/news/politics-and-nation/breach-at-kudankulam-nuclear-plant-may-have-gone-undetected-for-over-six-months-group-ib/articleshow/79412969.cms

Cosmos bank heist (2018)

Year	2018, India
Entity	Cosmos Bank, India
Business	Banking services
Attacker	Attack was attributed to Lazarus group of North Korea
Impact	Several cloned bank debit cards used for thousands of ATM transactions across India and 28 other countries in a 7-hour period on August 11, 2018. Parallel to that was SWIFT transfers. Total impact amounted to INR 94cr ($13.5 m)
Read More	https://www.hindustantimes.com/cities/15-months-later-no-lead-in-rs-94-cr-cosmos-bank-cyber-fraud-case/story-Ar6lk69HLJmBEyt9jGsx0K.html

Incidentally co-author Rohit Srivastwa was one of the investigators for this case. He was part of the Special Investigation Team (SIT) formed by Mumbai Police special branch.

Equifax Data Breach (2017)

Year	2017, USA
Entity	Equifax, USA
Business	Provides credit score information
Attacker	Threat actors exploited a vulnerability in Equifax's web application
Impact	Attackers gained unauthorized access to 147 million customers sensitive personal information (Name, SSN#, birthdates etc) leading to widespread data theft and financial fraud.
Read More	https://en.wikipedia.org/wiki/2017_Equifax_data_breach

In this case co-author Aalok Karnik while based out of US was partially assisting during the investigation from his former employer at that time.

Mirai Botnet Attacks (2016)

Year	2016, USA
Entity	Internet infrastructure providers and websites, DNS services
Business	70+ businesses were impacted due to this. To name a few CNN, Twitter, Amazon, HBO, PayPal, Reddit, Starbucks, etc
Attacker	Mirai botnet comprised of a network of compromised IoT devices like CCTV cameras.
Impact	Large scale DDoS attack against prominent services & websites were disrupted affected millions of users globally.
Read More	https://www.secureblink.com/threat-research/mirai

Prominent Indian Data Breaches Reported

If we look back a few years, media has reported a lot of data breaches in India as well, to name a few:

Note: Remember that data breach stories are known to the public from media reports, news articles etc. In reality, there are at least 10x more such stories which never received media attention or were pushed under the carpet by the organization.

You feel that pushing under the carpet is a good option? In upcoming chapters you'll see why this is a really bad idea.

Chapter 2

What cyber risk? We are already secure.

There are two types of organizations, those that have been attacked and those that will be attacked. Best we can do is minimize the probability and impact of an attack when it occurs.

> ***It's a matter of when, not if.***

Today, no organization can claim or assume they are not vulnerable to cyber-attacks. On the contrary, they need to understand techno-business relationships:

- How does any business leverage technology?
- What security risks do those technologies have?

As a business leader, it is about spending time to understand these techno-business risks, initiate conversations with your IT, security, legal, and compliance teams. Cybersecurity may seem like a massive sinkhole of money at the first, but it will protect your organization in a multitude of manners which we shall explore in this book.

A customer provides their data to an organization with some trust and hope that the data will not be abused and stored safely. and it is of paramount importance that the trust be maintained.

Data privacy is not just a buzz word anymore, it is the law and keeping data secure is critical, not just your operational data but even that of your vendors, customers etc.

1. Ignorance is not always bliss

In the modern digital landscape, it's easy to fall into the comforting trap of thinking, "Nobody is going to attack us". Why would an attacker bother with our small or medium-sized enterprise when there are bigger fish to fry, right?

Leaving your front door unlocked in a quiet neighbourhood, assuming you're immune to threats of theft, can leave you vulnerable to unexpected intruders. Same is true for cybersecurity.

Let's explore the common misconceptions that leads us to believe we're off the cybercriminals' radar, and why even the smallest organization can become a target for malicious actors in the vast online wilderness.

So, grab your cyber sunscreen and get ready to shed some light on the myths surrounding cybersecurity – because when it comes to defending our businesses from cyber threats, ignorance is not bliss.

2. Reality check

Well, here's the reality check: cybercriminals don't discriminate based on the business size or operational scope. In today's interconnected world, every digital footprint is a potential goldmine for opportunistic attackers.

In fact, SME's and MSME's are often prime targets as they underestimate the likelihood of an attack. They may not realize but they still possess valuable assets – customer information, financial records, intellectual property, etc – that can be exploited for profit.

Remember, cybercriminals are constantly scanning for vulnerabilities to exploit – and no business, small or large, is immune to their tactics.

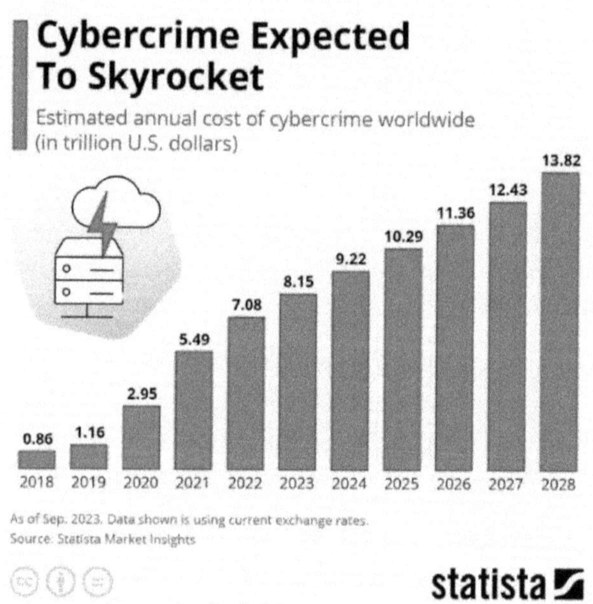

3. Knowledge is the First Line of Defence

Let's face it: cybercrime is a multi-billion-dollar industry fuelled by greed, opportunity, and a vast underground network of cybercriminals operating in the shadows of the internet often called as darknet.

From ransomware attacks crippling small businesses to phishing scams targeting unsuspecting individuals, the digital landscape is rife with threats lurking around every virtual corner.

Increasing the stakes are nation states keen on using cyber-attacks as a fifth dimension of warfare.

> **<u>Knowledge is power against cyber threats.</u>**
>
> By shedding light on the controls surrounding cybersecurity, we can arm ourselves with the tools and awareness needed to protect our digital assets and safeguard our businesses against potential threats.

It's time to take proactive steps to fortify our digital defences as best we can and protect our digital infrastructure.

Chapter 3

So where do we start?

It's easy to feel overwhelmed by the sheer magnitude of threats and vulnerabilities present today. As a business leader, you are tasked with being secure, staying compliant, and operating smoothly.

So, the question inevitably arises: where do we start?

It all starts with the right thought process.

As a business leader, you should be aware that cybersecurity is all about effective risk management. Adopting the right strategy combined with on-ground tactics will help mitigate the impact of any attack.

1. Cybersecurity is a business enabler

The journey towards cyber resilience begins with a fundamental shift in mindset – from viewing cybersecurity as a mere afterthought to embracing it as a strategic priority integral to the success and sustainability of your business.

It's crucial to recognize that cybersecurity is not just a technical issue – it's a business imperative. Just as you wouldn't neglect office ambience beautification or physical security measures like locks and alarms to protect your physical assets, neglecting cybersecurity puts your organization's digital assets and reputation at risk.

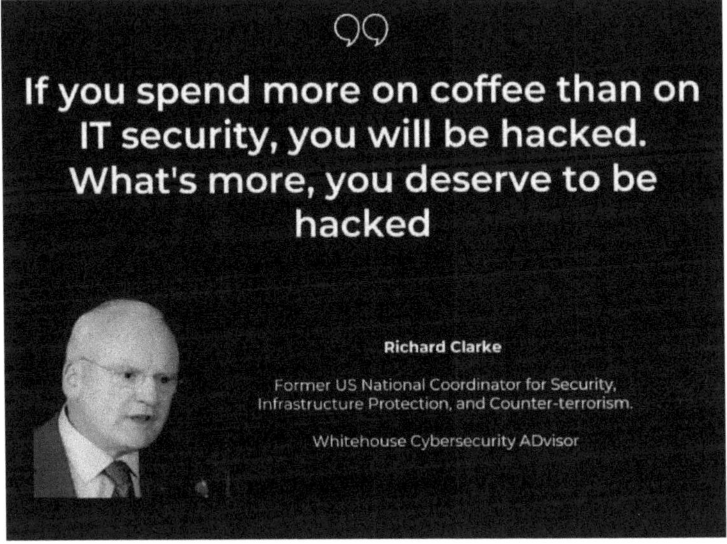

2. Assess your cybersecurity posture

With this newfound perspective in mind, the next step is to assess your organization's current cybersecurity posture. This involves conducting a comprehensive risk assessment to identify potential threats compromising the confidentiality, integrity, and availability of your data and systems.

The assessment should encompass all aspects of your organization's operations, from network infrastructure, software applications to employee practices and third-party relationships.

It's best to get this done from an outsider like a Virtual CISO to avoid an inherent "*organizational historical bias*" and have a fresh pair of eyes review your operations and provide relevant guidance.

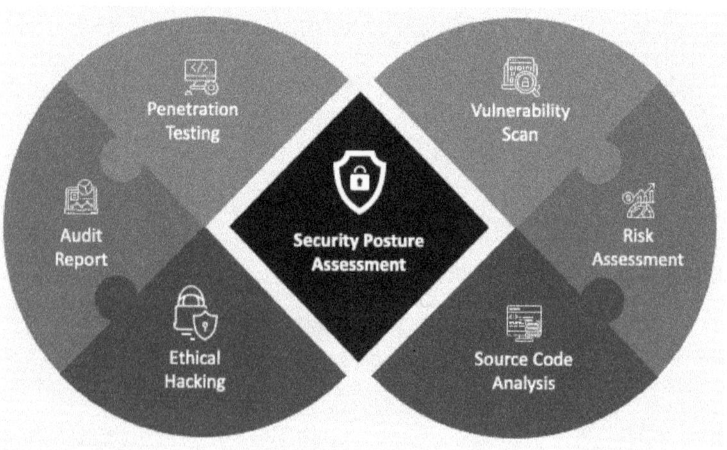

3. Develop a security roadmap

Once you have a clear understanding of your organization's cybersecurity risks, the next step is to develop a tailored & prioritized cybersecurity strategy and roadmap.

Align it with your organization's overall business objectives and risk appetite, outlining specific goals, priorities, and action plans to enhance your cybersecurity defences and resilience over time.

This may include investing in technology solutions, adopting security policies and procedures, and providing ongoing employee training and awareness programs.

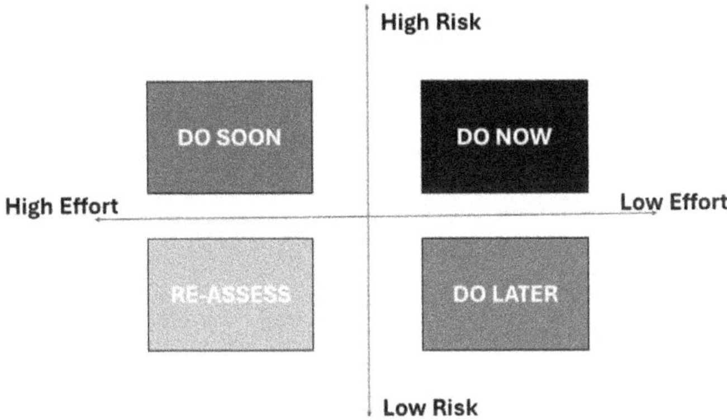

Do Now	Must within this quarter
Do Soon	Within next few quarters
Do Later	May be next year
Re-Assess	Review after high priority tasks done

4. PPT Methodology

Remember it's all about PPT – People Process and Technology. Adopting the right policies and processes helps in reducing technology expenses.

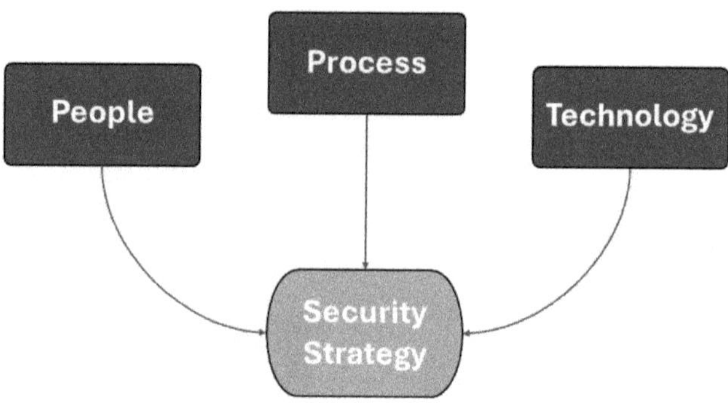

To achieve a resilient cyber security program, it is essential to establish a right balance of

- Leadership
- Governance
- Team capabilities
- Robust processes
- Adoption of industry guidelines
- Right set of technology tools

5. Collaborate across the organization

Business leaders must leverage team collaboration and communication as key pillars of an effective cybersecurity governance program.

This will assist you in better integrating cybersecurity across all your organization's operations and decision-making processes.

Internal Collaboration

Regular communication, reporting, and discussion on cybersecurity matters, including updates on cyber threats, incidents, and mitigation efforts, helps create a security focussed culture.

External Collaboration

Apart from internal collaboration, remember external collaboration is essential to:

- **Engage** with external partners and stakeholders, such as industry peers, government agencies, and cybersecurity experts.
- **Share** information and best practices by participating in tech forums and industry initiatives.

All this can enhance your organization's cyber resilience and readiness to respond to emerging threats and challenges.

6. Culture of Cyber Security Awareness

Ultimately, building a strong cybersecurity foundation requires a holistic approach:

- Encompass people, processes, and technology
- Create a culture of cybersecurity awareness and accountability
- Invest in the right tools and resources
- Establish effective governance and collaboration mechanisms

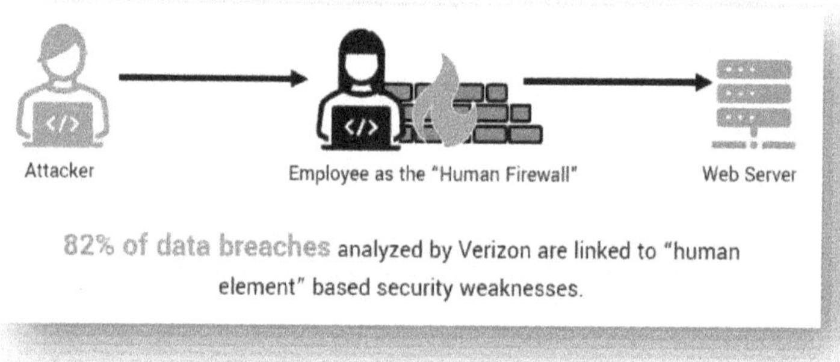

Source: https://www.thesslstore.com/blog/19-security-awareness-statistics-you-should-know-before-offering-training/

Chapter 4

What are the must haves in my strategy?

In the ever-evolving landscape of cybersecurity, laying a solid foundation is paramount to effectively navigate the complexities of the digital realm.

As a business leader, spearheading your organization's cybersecurity efforts requires a strategic approach encompassing:

- Proactive detection measures
- Responsive deterrent actions.

Key Strategies for Cyber Risk Management

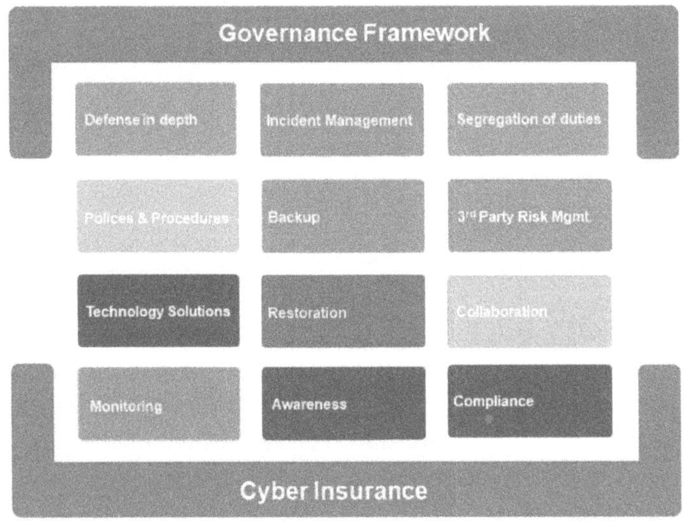

1. Governance Framework

Implementing a strong governance framework for cybersecurity involves establishing clear roles, responsibilities, and accountability mechanisms across all levels of the organization.

This begins with the formation of a dedicated "security steering committee" comprising representatives from diverse functional areas including finance, HR, legal, and compliance to gain valuable insights into the business and human-related aspects of security governance.

The security steering committee plays a crucial role to:

- Oversee and manage cybersecurity efforts
- Align business objectives and regulatory requirements
- Be a forum for discussing security-related issues, make strategic decisions, and resource allocation
- Establish communication channels for timely information flow
- Create reporting structures for accountability and transparency

Wrap-Up

Overall, a well-rounded governance framework empowers organizations to proactively address cybersecurity challenges, mitigate risks, and enhance resilience.

By fostering collaboration and accountability across different departments and levels of the organization, businesses can strengthen their overall security posture and adapt to evolving threats effectively.

2. Defence in Depth

Defence in depth is the most important strategy you should incorporate. With the ever-rising sophistication in cyber-attacks, stronger security at multiple levels is highly recommended.

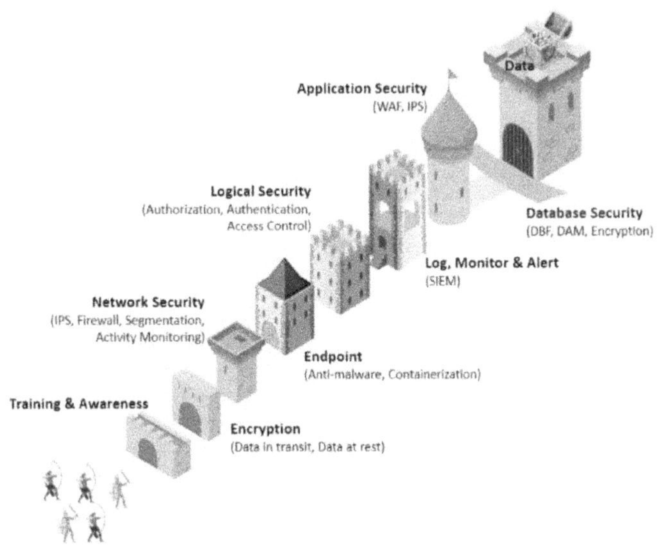

Source: https://blog.introduce.com.br/como-construir-um-arsenal-de-ferramentas-de-ciberseguranca-para-proteger-a-sua-empresa/

Defence in depth involves the following concepts:

- Deploying multiple layers of security controls across an organization's IT infrastructure. to protect against a wide range of cyber threats.
- No single security measure available in the market is failproof.
- A combination of complementary defences is needed to mitigate risks effectively.
- It minimizes the likelihood of a successful cyber-attack.

- Reduces the impact of security breaches by making it more difficult for adversaries to penetrate their defences and access sensitive data or systems.

For example, an antivirus protection is available at email server level, corporate firewall level but you still have an antivirus solution on the end point.

Wrap-Up

Defence in depth is not a one-time effort but an ongoing process that requires continual evaluation, adaptation, and improvement to effectively address evolving threats and risks.

3. Cybersecurity Policies and Procedures

Develop and implement robust policies and procedures to help decision-making regarding cybersecurity best practices, data protection, incident response, compliance requirements and guide employees' behaviour.

This would require collaboration between internal teams and external consultants to strike a right balance between security and usability tailored for your business landscape.

Take help from your vCISO in creating business appropriate policies and procedures.

If you have already a drafted set of policies, review the same.

**10 must-have information security policies
for every organization**

1	Acceptable use policy	6	Remote access policy
2	Network security policy	7	Vendor management policy
3	Data management policy	8	Removable media policy
4	Access control policy	9	Incident response policy
5	Password management policy	10	Security awareness and training policy

4. Technology Solutions

After a meticulous gap assessment, roadmap planning, and setting up right policy and procedure, the next step is to invest in robust cybersecurity technologies and solutions to detect, prevent, and respond to cyber threats effectively.

There are a few must haves from security point of view:

- End Point Protection
- Web Application Firewall
- Multi-factor Authentication
- Data encryption (at rest and in motion)
- SIEM
- More...

These may vary based on the security needs and compliance requirements of your organization. Speak to your CISO or Virtual CISO to identify your must-haves.

5. Continuous Monitoring and Improvement

Beware that adopting policies and procuring the latest technologies and platforms will not protect you to the fullest. Value from deployed security controls will be visible when mechanisms for continuous monitoring, testing, and improvement of cybersecurity controls, policies, and procedures are implemented.

A continuous monitoring cycle will provide visibility into network usage. This can be levelled up by fine-tuning the logging and monitoring environment.

A well-oiled monitoring process will surely help in decision making about capacity management, resource management, and funds allocation.

Monitoring is a Regulatory Guideline

This may sound repetitive, but we can't emphasis more on its importance, given that monitoring is a part of regulatory guidelines. An organization is expected to report identified cyber security issues to the regulator at the earliest. The reporting timeframe will differ based on the regulatory requirement.

Leverage Threat Intelligence Feeds

This will provide your organization with that extra edge to identify attack patterns from other sources. Efforts can be focussed such that certain attack vectors can be proactively covered ahead of time.

6. Incident Management Plan

Create a formalized Incident Management plan outlining procedures for detecting, responding to, and recovering from cybersecurity incidents, permitting swift and coordinated actions to mitigate breaches / disruption impact.

Source: https://devtools.in/blog/what-is-incident-management/

Communicate the incident management plan to everyone in the organisation facilitating the right action at the right time in case they see something wrong.

Print the relevant contact information or call tree and display it prominently at various places within the organisation.

7. Backup (3-2-1 Strategy)

The 3-2-1 backup strategy is an industry approach to data backup and disaster recovery, we strongly recommend checking with your team if you follow the same.

This strategy involves creating:

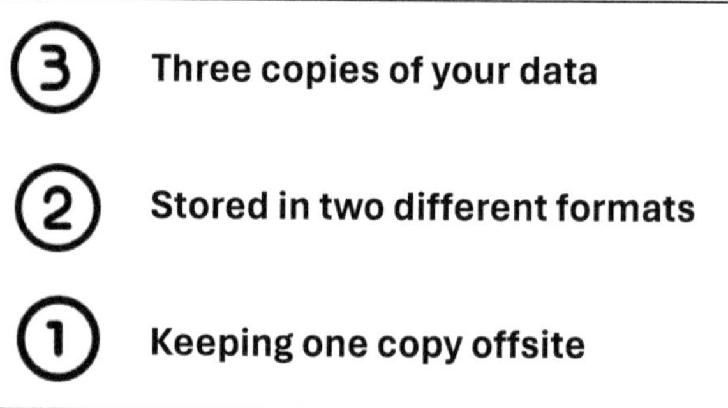

By adhering to this principle, organizations can mitigate the risk of data loss due to various threats, including hardware failures, malware attacks, and natural disasters.

Multiple data copies	Redundancy and availability
Multiple storage formats	Flexibility and protection against several types of failures
Offsite storage	Protects against localized disasters, such as fires or floods, compromising onsite backups

8. Data Restoration

Restoration testing is a crucial complimentary practise of backup and recovery systems. It involves simulating real-world scenarios where data or systems are lost or compromised and then initiating the restoration process to recover the lost data or restore the affected systems.

Backup is considered as the only sure shot recovery strategy from a ransomware attack. Restoration testing helps validate the integrity and reliability of backup data, ensuring that it can be successfully recovered in the event of a disaster.

By regularly conducting restoration tests, organizations can evaluate the effectiveness and efficiency of their backup and recovery procedures, identify any weaknesses or gaps in their systems, and refine their incident response plans accordingly.

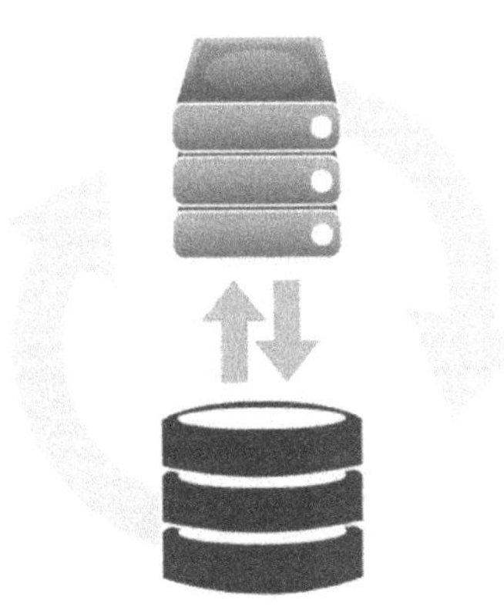

9. Employee Training and Awareness

An uninformed user could be your weakest link and it would be prudent to educate employees about common threats, best practices, and their roles and responsibilities in safeguarding sensitive information and systems.

The following programs will equip users with the knowledge of what to do when they encounter any fraud activity or an actual security issue.

1	Conduct regular training sessions on cybersecurity best practices
2	Implement simulated phishing exercises to educate employees about email security
3	Provide resources like posters, emails, and newsletters to reinforce key cybersecurity concepts
4	Encourage the use of strong, unique passwords and enable multi-factor authentication
5	Establish clear policies regarding data protection and safe internet usage
6	Foster a culture of reporting security incidents and suspicious activities
7	Offer incentives or recognition for employees who demonstrate good cybersecurity habits
8	Keep employees informed about the latest cyber threats and vulnerabilities
9	Conduct cybersecurity assessments and provide feedback to improve awareness
10	Promote a sense of accountability by assigning roles and responsibilities for cybersecurity tasks

10.   Segregation of Duties

Distribute duties and responsibilities among different individuals or teams within the organization on lines of maker-checker principle to:

Reduces Insider Threats	By separating tasks, no single individual has complete control, minimizing the risk of internal abuse or malicious activity.
Enhances Accountability	SoD ensures that multiple individuals are involved in critical processes, making it easier to trace actions and hold responsible parties accountable.
Mitigates Errors and Fraud	With distinct roles, errors or fraudulent activities are less likely to go unnoticed or be covered up, improving detection and prevention.
Strengthens Control Framework	Forms a foundational element of a robust control framework, enhancing overall security posture and compliance with regulations.
Supports Incident Response	Clear role delineation facilitates quicker and more effective incident response by streamlining investigation and resolution processes.

For example, IT systems changes to be done by one person/team and review audit of the same by security personnel/team/vCISO.

11.   Third-Party Risk Management (TPRM)

Every organization has some activities outsourced; these third-party vendors could be the biggest source of attack on your organization. Remember how an air conditioner vendor caused a data breach at Target, a large supermarket chain in US.

Assess and manage cybersecurity risks associated with third-party vendors, suppliers, and partners by implementing due diligence processes, contractual obligations, and security requirements.

TPRM is essential since an attack on a third party's infrastructure could result in a data breach and expose your data too.

Ideally, from a cyber security standpoint, your TPRM process should include:

12. Collaboration and Information Sharing

Foster collaboration and information sharing with industry peers, government agencies, and cybersecurity organizations to stay informed about emerging threats, best practices, and industry trends.

This can and should be done at various levels of the organization. Tactical teams should collaborate with tactical communities and leadership should network in their realms.

Large industry players and market leaders often share tactical threat intelligence, best practices, and more at a tactical level to help each other in achieving the larger goal - securing customer environments.

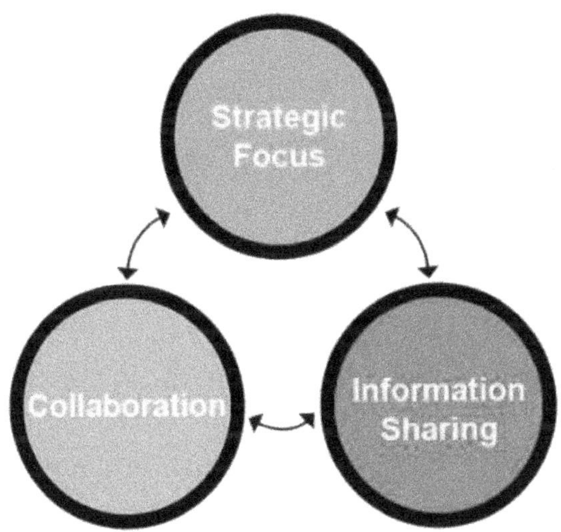

13. Regulatory Compliance

Compliance will be either asked by an industry regulator or a client. It's advised to be compliant with relevant cybersecurity regulations, standards, and frameworks applicable to your industry and geographic location, such as GDPR, HIPAA, PCI DSS, NIST, ISO 27001, and others.

Name	Description
ISO 27001 (Infosec Management)	Sets out the specification for an effective ISMS. Helps organizations protect their sensitive information through a comprehensive set of security controls and best practices, ensuring confidentiality, integrity, and availability of data.
SOC2 (Trust Service Criteria)	Framework for auditing and reporting on the controls at service organizations relevant to security, availability, processing integrity, confidentiality, and privacy. Specifies how organizations should manage customer data
HIPAA (Health Data)	Health Insurance Portability and Accountability Act, a U.S. legislation that sets standards for the security and privacy of protected health information (PHI)
PCI-DSS (Payment Data)	Comprehensive set of global security standards designed to protect financial data and enhance digital payment security.
GDPR (Privacy)	General Data Protection Regulation, an EU regulation that aims to protect the privacy and data of EU citizens and residents.
DPDP (Privacy)	Data protection that aims to regulate the processing of personal data of individuals in India.
CPRA (Privacy)	A U.S. state law enhancing privacy rights and consumer protection for California residents.

14. Cyber Insurance

In life we add a layer of protection by taking insurance, similarly, obtaining cyber insurance coverage can mitigate financial losses and liabilities associated with cybersecurity incidents. In Risk Management terminology, this is Risk Transfer.

Note: Cyber Insurance like any other market insurance has a cost premium associated via an underwriter. You as an organization is expected to maintain a certain minimum security maturity level to be insured and obtain the payout when the need arises.

Think of it this way, your health insurance premium will be higher if you are a smoker, frequent drinker, and have a history of cardiovascular disease. If your illness is attributed to heavy drinking / cardiac arrest, the underwriter could deny the insurance claim on count of negligence.

> **Cyber insurance is not a substitute for cyber resilience.**

Wrap-Up

These must-have strategies form the cornerstone of a comprehensive cybersecurity strategy, providing a framework for organizations to proactively identify, assess, and mitigate cybersecurity risks.

This fosters a culture of resilience, accountability, and collaboration across the enterprise.

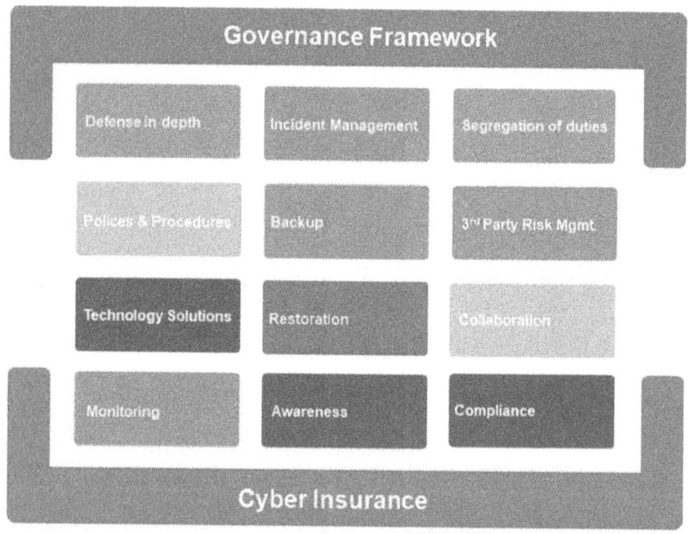

Chapter 5

Can my IT team take care of it?

It's easy to fall into the trap of complacency when you have a dedicated IT team who you think are capable of handling cybersecurity issues given, they manage a firewall and an antivirus.

While it's true that having a skilled and capable team is essential, relying solely on their expertise can leave your organization vulnerable to advanced techniques, emerging threats, and evolving risks.

Your IT and/or cybersecurity team may be skilled and dedicated but are not infallible.

1. Management buy-in is essential

Let's get one thing straight. Management approves funds permitting deployment of security controls. It is critical for you as a business leader to understand the rationale behind this investment.

Without your oversight and guidance, the team may overlook critical business risks or fail to adapt quickly to combat emerging threats.

Management's domain knowledge
Provides valuable business insights and perspectives complementing the IT team's technical expertise, ensuring a more holistic approach to cybersecurity.

Management's active involvement
Sends a powerful message demonstrating leadership's commitment to prioritizing cybersecurity as a strategic business enabler. Sets the tone for the entire organization and fosters a culture of security awareness and accountability.

Wrap-Up:

If you are unfamiliar with the information security domain, continue reading this book and/or you may want to onboard an external virtual CISO to assist in identifying your immediate risks.

2. Ask questions

How can you, as a business leader, upskill your domain knowledge and guide your team on the right path?

Answer to that is by asking the right questions and challenging your team to continually improve and innovate.

Here are some questions we suggest that business leaders should ask their IT team, C-Suite, or your trusted vCISO.

Governance	What industry standards and best practices are we following?
	How can we improve?
	What is our coverage percentage as of today?
	How do we measure the effectiveness of our cybersecurity program?
	What metrics do we use to track progress and performance?

Policies	Have our policies been enforced across the organization?
	How can we make it better?
	What percentage of controls have we onboarded and what controls need to be implemented?

<table>
<tr><td>Incident Response</td><td>How do we respond if we undergo a data breach?

When was our incident response plan reviewed?

What is our Mean Time To Detect (MTTD) and Mean Time To Recover (MTTR)?</td></tr>
<tr><td>People</td><td>What percentage of our employees are susceptible to social engineering attack?

What current / future investments towards training and awareness programs will educate employees to recognize and respond to security threats?

Are the employees facing trouble after implementing certain security controls?</td></tr>
<tr><td>Vendor Management</td><td>Which 3rd parties access our data?

What controls have we placed on them?

Who are our riskiest 3rd parties when it comes to data security?

Have we reviewed our data sharing confidentiality agreement with them?</td></tr>
<tr><td>Technology</td><td>What are our most critical assets we need to protect?

How have we protected our cloud assets, Websites?

What is the Mean Time To Acknowledge (MTTA) of our company?

How can we improve our Mean Time Between Failure (MTBF)?</td></tr>
</table>

Remember such questions can also be directed to other departments like legal, HR, and compliance teams.

By actively engaging with your cybersecurity team and asking these probing questions:

- You can challenge them to think critically, innovate, and continuously improve, driving your organization to new heights of cybersecurity excellence.
- You can help them stay ahead of the curve and help your organization remain resilient in the face of evolving threats.

Chapter 6

What is Cyber Risk Management?

One of the key tools used in effective risk management is the Risk Register, a comprehensive repository that documents identified risks, their attributes, and the strategies employed to address them.

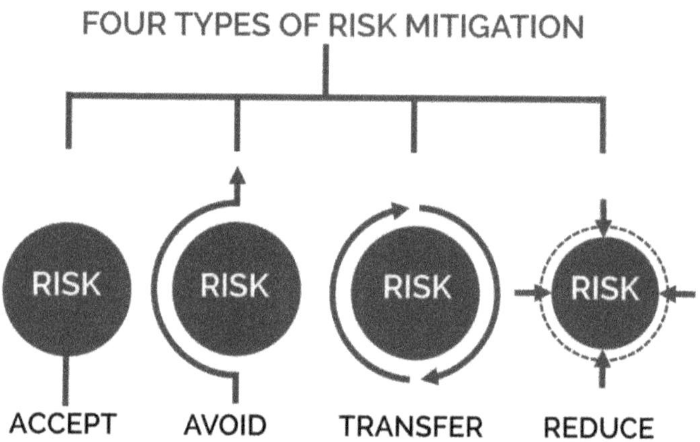

Risks can be handled in 4 ways:

- Accept the risk and continue business as usual
- Avoid the risk and accept the consequences of an attack
- Transfer the risk and liability to a third party entity
- Reduce the risk to an acceptable operational degree

1. Risk Components

Risk Identification

At the core of risk measurement is the process of risk identification, where potential risks are systematically identified and documented. This can be achieved through various techniques, including risk workshops, scenario analysis, and historical data review.

By engaging stakeholders from different departments and levels of the organization, a comprehensive list of risks can be compiled, ensuring that no potential threat goes unnoticed.

Risk Assessment

Once risks are identified, they must be assessed to determine their significance and prioritize them for mitigation. Risk assessment involves evaluating:

- Likelihood of a risk occurring
- Potential impact it could have on the organization

Techniques such as risk scoring, and scenario analysis can help quantify risks and prioritize them based on their severity and potential consequences.

Conduct regular and comprehensive assessments to identify and prioritize cybersecurity risks across your organization's systems, processes, and people.

To avoid "organizational historical bias", this is best done by a third-party entity. Opt for a vendor agnostic team to tell you what you need, not what a vendor can sell.

Risk Quantification

Quantify your risks in money terms to understand financial impact of being secure. You can leverage FAIR model here, that provides a framework for breaking down risk into measurable factors and using statistics and probabilities to estimate risk in quantitative terms.

Risk Treatment

After assessing risks, organizations must develop strategies to address them effectively. This is where risk treatment comes into play, encompassing various approaches such as risk mitigation, risk transfer, risk avoidance, and risk acceptance.

By implementing controls and measures to reduce the likelihood or impact of risks, organizations can minimize their exposure and enhance their resilience to cyber threats.

Risk Monitoring

Continuous monitoring and review of the risk register are critical to ensuring its accuracy and effectiveness over time. Risks are dynamic and can change rapidly in response to internal and external factors.

Therefore, it is essential to periodically:

- Review the risk register
- Update risk assessments
- Adjust risk treatment strategies

This ensures that the risk register remains relevant and aligned with the organization's risk appetite and business objectives.

Implementing effective risk register management practices is essential for maximizing the value of the risk register via:

- Establishing clear roles and responsibilities for maintaining the risk register
- Leveraging technology tools to streamline the risk management process
- Fostering a culture of accountability and transparency around risk management.

Risk Prioritization

Prioritizing risks is essential to allocate resources effectively and focus efforts where they will have the most significant impact.:

- Potential impact and probability of occurrence
- Organizational risk appetite and tolerance

Potential Impact and Probability of Occurrence

Risks with a high likelihood of occurring and a severe impact on the organization's operations, reputation, or financial health should be prioritized for immediate attention.

This may include vulnerabilities in critical systems or processes, emerging threats that exploit known weaknesses, or regulatory compliance gaps that pose significant legal or financial risks.

Organizational risk appetite and tolerance

Some risks may be acceptable within certain thresholds, while others may be deemed unacceptable and require immediate mitigation efforts.

By aligning risk prioritization with the organization's strategic objectives and tolerance for risk, business leaders can make informed decisions about where to invest resources and how to best protect the organization from cyber threats.

This strategic approach aligns cybersecurity efforts with business priorities and can effectively mitigate the most significant risks to the organization's success.

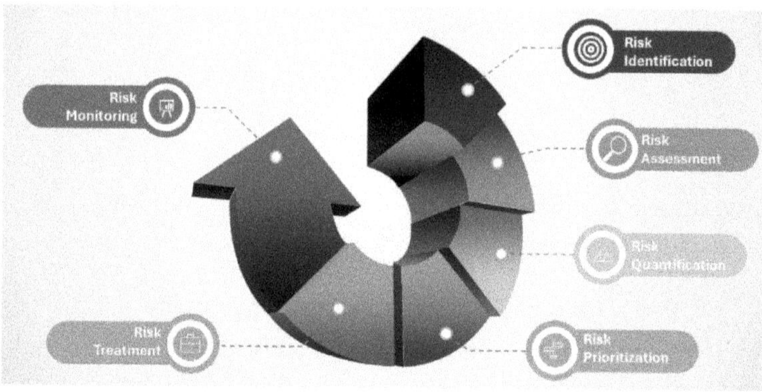

2. What is a Risk Register?

The risk register serves as a central hub for managing risks across the organization, providing stakeholders with visibility into potential threats and the measures in place to mitigate them.

However, to derive maximum value from the risk register, it is essential to understand its components and the processes involved in its management.

Chapter 7

Does moving to "Cloud" make me secure?

Cloud is as secure as much you configure it to be and as much as you pay for

Many business leaders believe that migrating to the cloud is the ultimate solution for security, assuming that cloud providers inherently offer the highest level of protection. While cloud providers do implement robust security measures, this perception can be misleading.

Cloud security is not automatically assured by merely shifting to the cloud; it is a shared responsibility. The cloud provider is responsible to secure the infrastructure, but the organization is responsible to configure and manage its applications, data, and user access as per industry guidelines.

Misconfigurations, inadequate access controls, and failure to adhere to best practices can expose sensitive data to breaches and unauthorized access.

Securing cloud environments requires a proactive and well-informed approach.

Responsibility	On-Prem	IaaS	PaaS	SaaS
Data classification & accountability				
Client & end-point protection				
Identity & access management				
Application level controls				
Network controls				
Host infrastructure				
Physical security				

Cloud Customer   Cloud Provider

On-Prem	In your physical custody
IaaS	Infrastructure as a Service
PaaS	Platform as a Service
SaaS	Software as a Service

1. Provider best practices

Cloud providers like AWS, Microsoft Azure, and Google Cloud Platform implement a comprehensive set of security practices to safeguard their infrastructure.

These practices form the backbone of a secure cloud environment, but they also require active participation and understanding from their clients to be effective.

Amazon's AWS	Well Architected Review
Google's GCP	Cloud Architecture Framework
Microsoft's Azure	Well Architected Review

The provider best practices are designed to help organizations build secure, high-performing, resilient, and efficient infrastructure for their applications. It focuses on five key pillars:

- Operational excellence
- Security
- Reliability
- Performance efficiency
- Cost optimization

Operational Excellence

Providers encourage the use of automation and continuous integration/continuous deployment (CI/CD) pipelines to maintain consistent and secure operations. This includes automated patch management, regular security assessments, and incident response automation.

Security

Providers emphasizes the importance of a shared responsibility model where they secure the cloud infrastructure, while customers secure the data and applications they run on the cloud.

Numerous security tools and features, including identity and access management (IAM), encryption options, network security measures, configurations, and security monitoring and logging services are provided for the same.

Reliability

Given the obvious nature of criticality, providers offer comprehensive services for data backup, disaster recovery, multi-region deployments, and maintaining system availability to enhance reliability.

Performance Efficiency

Providers suggests leveraging the right resources for the right tasks, optimizing performance and cost. This involves using scalable and flexible resources, load balancing, and efficient data storage solutions.

Cost Optimization

Providers understand the need for cost transparency since all cloud services have an associated cost. They provide tools to monitor and control costs for efficient resource management and allowing the client to determine a cost-effective service choices

This help in optimizing expenses without compromising security.

Wrap-Up

Following these best practices ensures that the cloud infrastructure is robust, secure, and efficient.

However, it is vital for businesses to not solely rely on providers but to integrate these practices with their own security strategies to create a holistic security posture.

2. Industry best practices

Apart from following cloud provider best practices, it is essential to adhere to industry best practices to maintain a secure cloud environment. These practices are established through a combination of expert consensus, compliance requirements, and lessons learned from security incidents across various industries.

Here are key industry best practices that should be integrated into any cloud security strategy:

Adopt a Zero Trust Model

The Zero Trust security model operates on a "Trust No One" policy.

It assumes that threats can come from both inside and outside the network. This approach requires strict identity verification for every person, service, and device attempting to access resources, regardless of their location.

Implementing Zero Trust involves continuous monitoring and validation, enforcing least-privilege access, and segmenting networks to limit the lateral movement of attackers.

Encryption Everywhere

Having data encrypted both in transit and at rest is a fundamental best practice. Industry standards recommend using strong encryption protocols

Data at Rest	AES-256
Data in Motion	TLS 1.2 / 1.3

Additionally, key management practices should be robust, ensuring that encryption keys are securely stored and rotated regularly. Cloud providers even permit the flexibility of BYOK (Bring Your Own Key) and encrypt data via customer keys.

Regular Audits and Assessments

Conducting regular security audits and vulnerability assessments helps identify and mitigate risks. These assessments should include penetration testing, configuration reviews, and compliance checks against standards such as ISO 27001, NIST Cybersecurity Framework, and CIS Controls.

Incident Response Planning

Developing and maintaining a comprehensive incident response plan is crucial. This plan should outline procedures for detecting, responding to, and recovering from security incidents. Regularly testing and updating the incident response plan ensures preparedness and minimizes the impact of breaches.

Third-Party Risk Management

Engaging third-party vendors introduces additional risks. It's essential to conduct thorough due diligence and ongoing monitoring of third-party security practices.

This includes reviewing their security policies, and enforcing they comply with relevant standards, and incorporating security requirements into contracts.

Security Awareness Training

Regular training programs for employees are vital in fostering a security-conscious culture. Training should cover topics such as phishing awareness, secure coding practices, and recognizing social engineering tactics.

Keeping the workforce informed about the latest threats and best practices helps in preventing security incidents.

Adherence to Regulatory Requirements

Compliance with regulatory standards like GDPR, HIPAA, and PCI-DSS is non-negotiable. These regulations often encompass specific security measures that organizations must implement to protect sensitive data.

Regular compliance audits ensure that the organization meets these regulatory requirements.

Use of Advanced Security Technologies

Leveraging advanced security tools such as Security Information and Event Management (SIEM) systems, Endpoint Detection and

Response (EDR), and Artificial Intelligence (AI)-driven threat detection enhances security capabilities.

These tools provide real-time monitoring, threat intelligence, and automated responses to potential threats.

Shared Responsibility Model

Understanding and implementing the shared responsibility model is crucial. While cloud providers secure the underlying infrastructure, it's the responsibility of the organization to secure their data, applications, and configurations.

Clearly delineating these responsibilities helps prevent security gaps.

Wrap-Up

By integrating these industry best practices, organizations can significantly enhance their cloud security posture, ensuring a robust defense against evolving threats.

These practices, combined with provider-specific measures and internal strategies, create a comprehensive approach to cloud security.

3. Business best practices

Implementing business-specific best practices for cloud security ensures that an organization's unique needs and objectives are met while maintaining robust security. Here are essential business best practices to consider:

Develop a Cloud Security Policy

Establish a comprehensive cloud security policy tailored to your business's needs is crucial. This policy should outline acceptable use, data protection measures, access controls, and incident response procedures.

Ensuring all employees understand and adhere to this policy helps create a consistent security framework.

Conduct Regular Training and Awareness Programs

Cloud security is also a shared responsibility that involves every employee. Regular training programs should be conducted to educate staff about the latest threats, secure use of cloud services, and best practices for data protection.

Tailored training sessions can address specific roles, such as developers, administrators, and general users, ensuring everyone is equipped to contribute to the organization's security posture.

This will enforce a security-first culture within the organization.

Implement Strong Access Controls

Strict access controls based on the principle of least privilege is vital. Role-based access control (RBAC) ensures that employees only have access to the data and systems necessary for their roles.

Multi-factor authentication (MFA) adds an extra layer of security, protecting against unauthorized access. For cloud administrative accounts access them only via bastion hosts (jump servers) with restricted usage and monitor the activity on those accounts.

Perform Regular Security Assessments

Conducting regular security assessments, including penetration testing and vulnerability scanning, helps identify and address potential weaknesses.

These assessments should be part of a continuous improvement process, with findings integrated into the security strategy and remediation efforts promptly executed.

Data Classification and Protection

Classifying data according to its sensitivity and applying appropriate protection measures is essential. This involves encrypting sensitive data, implementing data loss prevention (DLP) solutions, and monitoring data access and usage patterns to detect and prevent unauthorized activities.

Monitor and Log Activity

Continuous monitoring and logging of cloud activities help detect and respond to suspicious behaviour. Implementing Security Information and Event Management (SIEM) solutions allows for real-time analysis and correlation of security events, enabling swift incident detection and response.

Backup and Recovery Planning

Regularly backing up data and having a tested disaster recovery plan ensures business continuity in case of data loss or security incidents.

The 3-2-1 backup strategy (three copies of data, on two different media, with one copy off-site) is a recommended in cloud as well approach to safeguard critical information.

Vendor Management and SLAs

When engaging with cloud service providers, it's important to manage vendor relationships carefully. Clearly defined Service Level Agreements (SLAs) should outline security expectations, responsibilities, and penalties for non-compliance.

Regular reviews of vendor performance and security practices help maintain a secure partnership.

Continuous Improvement and Adaptation

The threat landscape is constantly evolving, so businesses must continuously review and improve their security practices. Regularly updating security policies, adopting new technologies, and staying informed about emerging threats and trends are key to maintaining a strong security posture.

Wrap-Up

By following these business best practices, organizations can ensure a secure cloud environment that supports their operational goals while mitigating risks.

Combining these practices with provider-specific measures and industry standards creates a comprehensive and resilient security strategy.

Chapter 8

What about the budget?

Though we wish otherwise, budget is a limited (and very precious) resource. Leadership cannot write a blank check, but they need to approve an effective cybersecurity budget.

1. Key Considerations for a Cybersecurity budget

Compliance costs

Organizations that are subject to global or local regulatory mandates, such as HIPAA, GDPR or PCI-DSS, will have compliance-related costs such as audit preparation & reporting, hiring for qualified roles such as Data Protection Officer (DPO) and/or full time CISO.

Risk Perception

Budgets for every organization largely depends on the mindset of the leadership. Let's face it, leadership is the one holding the funds and unless they approve the budget the cybersecurity program is stagnant.

An often-overlooked point is that your budget could be subject to change given new clients or if the company commences operations in new geographies. Geopolitical upheavals can also change security perceptions and hence the security budget.

Hence it is critical to legitimately convince leadership that cyber threats to their organization are a reality and could happen anytime.

Software

This obvious expense typically includes multiple security solutions for specific security controls such as antimalware applications, asset management, firewalls, network monitoring, vulnerability assessment, auditing and change management tools, and backup and recovery solutions; to name a few.

Hardware

To complement the software security controls, certain on-premises footprint will need to be maintained. Allocate a budget to upgrade servers, routers, and other IT infrastructure. Additionally, do plan investments around workstations, laptops, conferencing, and other hardware.

Services

Engage third-party cybersecurity vendors to perform a tailored specific task such as vulnerability assessment, penetration testing, gap analysis, compliance audit, etc. Onboarding a vendor for a continual managed security service will help tighten your existing security controls.

Personnel

Hiring skilled personnel with relevant cybersecurity experience will be your biggest expense. Very often, the IT team head is assigned cybersecurity tasks, and the lack of knowledge and experience will lead to a vulnerable cybersecurity posture.

It is critical that you utilize cybersecurity personnel and assist them with deploying automated solutions.

This allows your security team to focus on strategy than getting bogged down in menial repetitive tasks. This will keep your cybersecurity posture in top shape.

Goes without saying this will help with personnel retention and morale upliftment.

Training programs

Provide security training to all users with access to your data and systems. Training programs could be imparted by an external agency or as part of your IT team's initiative.

Check the effectiveness of training programs via means such as phishing tests, certifications, etc.

Incident response

When successful cyberattacks do occur, the fiscal impact can range from minimal to bankruptcy. Given the wide impact range, it would be prudent to assign funds for handling various security incidents.

Costs can include forensic investigations, legal costs, compliance penalties, public relations efforts, and compensation measures like identity theft monitoring.

Cybersecurity insurance

A not so frequently discussed security cost is cybersecurity insurance. This is procured to mitigate the residual risks such as financial cost impact of a data breach. If your risk impact and threat perception is extremely high, then you could additionally purchase insurance along with other cybersecurity controls.

> ***Cyber Insurance needs a basic level of Cyber Security***

A critical point to note is that any cybersecurity insurance underwriter will expect you to be compliant with a basic level of security controls and they will assess your organization for the same.

If this criterion is not met the underwriter will label your organization as "high risk". This indicates high probability of a successful attack on your infrastructure. This will result in an increase of your insurance premium or rejection of providing coverage.

So, when purchasing insurance either spend on deploying security controls or be prepared for a high insurance premium.

Contingencies and unexpected costs

Even if you do buy cybersecurity insurance, consider some unforeseen expenses that insurance or even your security budget will not cover. Consider some buffer for unexpected expenses in your cybersecurity budget beyond all your listed items.

An effective way to explain this is discovery of vulnerabilities for which a patch is not yet released (AKA Zero Day) and there is significant effort involved to protect your organization from this vulnerability.

This effort could include procurement of a security solution, cloud storage, licensing, hiring personnel etc which was not included in your annual security budget.

Wrap-Up

Simply put, divide your cybersecurity budget on the following categories:

- Detection of intrusion attempts
- Containment of intrusions
- Recovery from intrusions
- Prevention of future intrusions
- Contingencies for future threats and Upgrade defences

Relevant software and hardware are needed to be managed by competent personnel or external services. Adopt robust security controls, technologies, and processes that operate together in a cohesive manner.

2. Cost-Benefit Analysis

Justifying a cybersecurity budget is extremely challenging simply because cybersecurity is not a tangible item that one can hold, touch, and feel to understand its complexity. It is ignored until an actual cyberattack occurs or a regulatory fine is imposed.

Business leaders should be proactive instead of being reactive about adopting cybersecurity best practices and defences.

> ***Cybersecurity is a Business Enabler***

Most business leaders do not understand that the cost of non-compliance is significantly higher than implementing security controls.

Scenario:

Your business is hit by a cyber-attack leading to data theft and subsequent leakage of PII data onto the dark web.

Business Impact:

Legal suits, drop in stock price or business valuation, regulatory costs, erosion of customer trust, last minute deployment of security controls, damage to company brand & credibility.

Financial Costs:

Lawyer fees, ransomware extortion payments (Don't do that), public relations fees, credit monitoring compensation to users, purchase of security controls above and beyond allocated budgets, systems/data restore costs, manpower effort to recover from attack.

Wrap-Up:

As a business leader, ask yourself this ... is skimping on cybersecurity expenses really worth the other costs you will incur later?

 - The compliance benefits achieved after onboarding security products will far outweigh the stress incurred with maintaining a non-compliant environment.

 - Consider both tangible and intangible costs and benefits (reduced risk exposure, improved operational efficiency, and enhanced customer trust).

3. Budget Planning, Forecasting and Allocation

Most firms will create an Annual Operations Planning (AOP) document containing their annual budget. Within this budget cybersecurity is often ignored or reduced to a minimum resulting in a vulnerable infrastructure.

Cybersecurity budget allocation involves striking a balance between budget appetite and risk appetite.

Strategies for developing a comprehensive cybersecurity budget plan, include setting budgetary goals, establishing timelines, and identifying resource requirements.

Consideration of cybersecurity trends, emerging threats, and technological advancements in budget forecasting.

Collaboration with key stakeholders including IT, finance, and executive leadership, in the budget planning process to ensure alignment with organizational objectives.

4. Procurement Cycles

Lengthy procurement cycles are the main reason for organizations to remain vulnerable for lengthy periods of time. As a business leader it is your job to:

- Initiate processes to identify vulnerabilities
- Identify solutions to mitigate vulnerabilities
- Approve budgets to purchase solutions
- Instruct IT dept to deploy solutions
- Review the actionable results derived from deployed solutions

Tying up the solution purchase in bureaucratic red tape and subsequently delaying its deployment will lead to a vulnerable environment.

Avoid this situation by actively involving yourself during the solution procurement stages and ensuring funds are approved leading to a timely deployment of the security control.

5. Licensing

Most software today is annually licensed SaaS, leading to a multiyear investment. Hardware on the other hand is purchased as a one-time investment. Certain solutions need hardware and software from the same vendor (e.g., backup solutions). Hardware vendors charge annual fees for their software to run on their hardware.

Updates are available for both software / security updates for hardware devices could be released at random times.

Image Credits: Labs64

6. Budget Size Constraint?

Honestly, there is no one size fits all industry formula or any number that can even come close to a practical budget. Certain factors will affect the budget size that you as a business leader will approve.

Organization Size

Large organizations will have larger IT footprints creating complex environments which are manually unmanageable. Certain quantum of software/hardware platforms will need to be adopted to maintain a secure environment.

Sector

Certain industry verticals and sectors, given their inherent familiarity with software platforms tend to allocate larger budgets for cybersecurity. Other industries might not have that luxury and tend to allocate smaller funds due to their inherent unfamiliarity with software platforms and adoption of security processes.

Compliance Requirements

Certain compliance requirements and mandates such as HIPAA, PCI-DSS are applicable to sectors operating in the healthcare and finance sectors, respectively. This will increase the security budget.

Security Maturity

Maturity level in an organization is dictated by how efficiently it has implements security controls, processes, and reporting. As a business leader, your question to your IT team should be ... *"When will I be attacked and how often?"*.

Like levels in a computer game, security maturity levels are achieved over time. Depending on how fast you want to reach a certain maturity level, your budget should reflect that speed.

Your organizations' maturity journey can start by referring to NIST CSF 2 (National Institute of Standards & Technology – Cyber Security Framework v2)

Maturity depends on maintaining a balance between the right number of proactive measures and reactive measures.

Risk Profile

The risk profile of an organization depends on its operations and data being stored.

Some organizations store, process sensitive data by operating in federal or military environments. For obvious reasons such facilities are high security facilities with controlled environments and strict access control.

Other organizations might store PII, health, or financial information, these will be deemed as regulated industries. The risks for such organizations would be different from the earlier example.

Mitigating risks in regulated versus low risk versus high-risk environments require different security controls to be deployed.

As we can clearly observe, the risk profile of an organization will directly dictate the budget amount.

Third party Vendor Risk

These vendors may not have the same cyber security goals, practices, and technology that you have. Outsourcing of IT tasks or operational processes will introduce an inherent risk that will need to be addressed via a TPRM process.

As a business leader, you should undertake initiatives to review the security controls for vendors with whom you share data.

Prior Incidents

A popular saying ... Once bitten twice shy. If your organization has experienced a cyber-attack in the future, chances are the budget for cybersecurity will be higher than the previous year. This is simply because the organization does not want to deal with the pain of data restoration, network traffic management etc.

For an IT dept to perform these tasks without automation is extremely time consuming and will increase the recovery time significantly.

Bearing the cost of downtime for an organization could be catastrophic in certain circumstances.

7. Capex vs. Opex

CapEx (Capital Expense) and OpEx (Operational Expense) are two distinct categories of expenditures that play a crucial role in any budgeting cycle. Today most software solutions migrate to OpEx model giving you the flexibility to choose another vendor in the event you cannot extract value from the currently deployed product.

CapEx may be more suitable when:

- Long term security infrastructure is needed for on-premises hardware deployments
- Greater control over the asset is needed especially in areas of handling sensitive data, purchase of endpoints
- Hiring resources to maintain infrastructure
- Compliance and Regulatory requirements
- On premise backup systems need deployment
- Long term contracts with vendors after evaluating exit clauses

OpEx may be more suitable when:

- Ongoing managed services / subscriptions where latest cutting-edge services are leveraged without large upfront cost
- SaaS platforms or cloud services are leveraged
- Outsourced activity to external vendors
- Short term contracts with vendors

Advisable to resolve critical regulatory issues first then move onto other high-risk items. Complete low effort activities quickly.

8. Open-Source Considerations

Free and Open-Source Software (FOSS) offers numerous benefits for organizations seeking cost-effective and flexible solutions to enhance their cybersecurity posture.

When incorporating FOSS into corporate environments it requires careful consideration of licensing requirements, security implications, ongoing maintenance, etc.

Key pointers to consider:

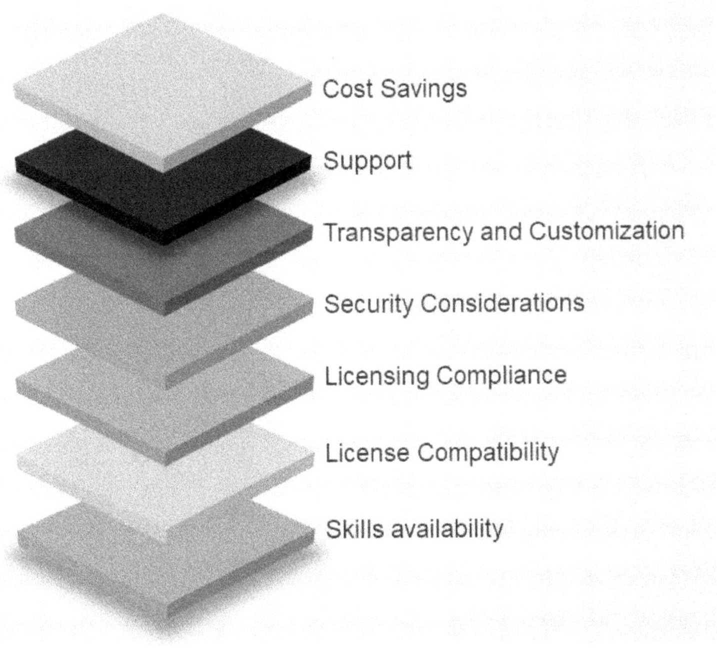

Cost Savings

A primary advantage of FOSS is its cost-effectiveness. Unlike proprietary solutions that often come with hefty licensing fees, open-source software is typically available for free, allowing organizations to allocate their budget more efficiently and invest in other areas of cybersecurity.

Free software looks great in a budget sheet and while justifying your security budget to other business leaders during cost benefit analysis discussions. However, it's important to consider few more things like:

- Hardware required to run the software
- Skilled workforce proficient in deploying and managing open source solutions
- Potential integration with currently deployed solutions

Support

Open-source projects benefit from a vibrant community of developers who contribute code, report bugs, and provide support. This collaborative approach leads to:

- Faster issue resolution
- Improved security
- Development of innovative features

However, it may not be as good as it sounds, since specialised software may not have right support available.

Transparency and Customization

The transparent nature of open-source software allows organizations to inspect the source code, identify vulnerabilities, and make custom modifications to suit their specific requirements.

This level of transparency can enhance trust and confidence in the security of the software, as organizations have greater visibility into its inner workings.

Security Considerations

While open-source software can offer significant security benefits, it is not immune to vulnerabilities and risks. Organizations must stay vigilant and proactive in monitoring security advisories, applying patches, and implementing best practices for secure configuration and deployment.

Additionally, overreliance on open-source components introduces dependencies that may pose security challenges if not managed effectively.

Myth: FOSS code has no vulnerabilities due to community review.

Reality: OpenSSL had a major vulnerability named Heartbleed that existed in OpenSSL code since December 2011. It remained undetected until April

Licensing Compliance

One critical consideration when using open-source software in corporate environments is compliance with licensing requirements.

Many open-source licenses, such as the GNU General Public License (GPL), impose certain obligations on organizations, such as making the source code of derivative works freely available to the public.

Failure to comply with these licensing terms can result in legal consequences, including lawsuits and damage to the organization's reputation.

License Compatibility

Some open-source licenses may be incompatible with the proprietary licenses of other software components used in the organization's infrastructure.

Organizations must carefully assess the licensing terms of open-source software and ensure compatibility with existing systems and applications to avoid conflicts and compliance issues.

Skills availability

One challenge organization's may encounter when considering open-source security solutions is the potential lack of skilled personnel proficient in their implementation and maintenance.

While open-source software offers cost-effective and flexible options for enhancing cybersecurity, deploying, and managing these solutions effectively requires specialized knowledge and expertise. Market demand for such expertise far outweighs the talent pool which could lead to difficulty in recruiting and retaining qualified personnel.

This shortage can hinder organizations' ability to fully leverage open-source security solutions capabilities. Building internal expertise to bridge this gap could mean investments in training initiatives via external agencies. and management of open-source security solutions.

Be aware that if your open-source resource vacates their role then you may have a tough time hiring new resources.

Wrap-Up

Successful adoption of open-source solutions and platforms needs a strong understanding of licensing, risk management, talent management. It is critical to hire capable, knowledgeable, and trusted staff to handle your open-source architecture.

Chapter 9

Anything specific for Cyber-Physical (OT/ICS) systems?

As technology continues to evolve, the integration of cyber-physical systems (commonly known as Operational Technology OT or Industrial Control System ICS) with the IT environment – has become increasingly prevalent across various industries, from manufacturing and healthcare to transportation, retail, and smart cities.

While OT offers numerous benefits, such as increased efficiency, automation, and real-time monitoring, they also introduce unique cybersecurity challenges and considerations.

Purdue Reference Architecture Model for OT/ICS Systems

This is the most widely used architecture framework for OT environments. Integrating cybersecurity here has its own challenges such as outdated hardware software combination, incompatibility with new protocols and more.

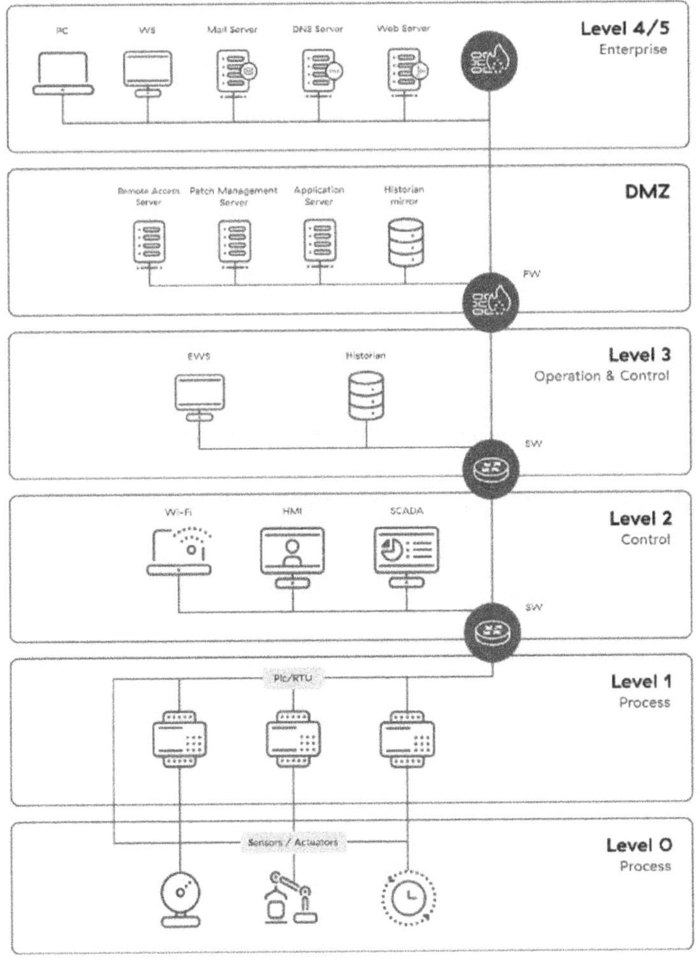
PC
WS
Mail Server
DNS Server
Web Server
Level 4/5
Enterprise
Remote Access Server
Patch Management Server
Application Server
Historian mirror
DMZ
FW
EWS
Historian
Level 3
Operation & Control
SW
Wi-Fi
HMI
SCADA
Level 2
Control
SW
Plc/RTU
Level 1
Process
Sensors / Actuators
Level 0
Process

Recommended Reading:

If you have an OT environment in your business, reading about STUXNET or watching a documentary on the same is highly recommended. It's absolutely fascinating to deep dive into how a sophisticated nation state attacks involves multiple attack vectors to carry out a successful cyber-attack on a nuclear power plant.

The STUXNET Story

It's also seen that lot of organizations keep an airgap between IT & OT to mitigate against this risk but here we'd like to bring your attention to the popular STUXNET attack where the weakness in the process caused an attack on Iranian nuclear enrichment plant at Natanz.

https://spectrum.ieee.org/the-real-story-of-stuxnet

To understand the complete story including the geo-politics, the documentary "Zero Days" is a must watch.

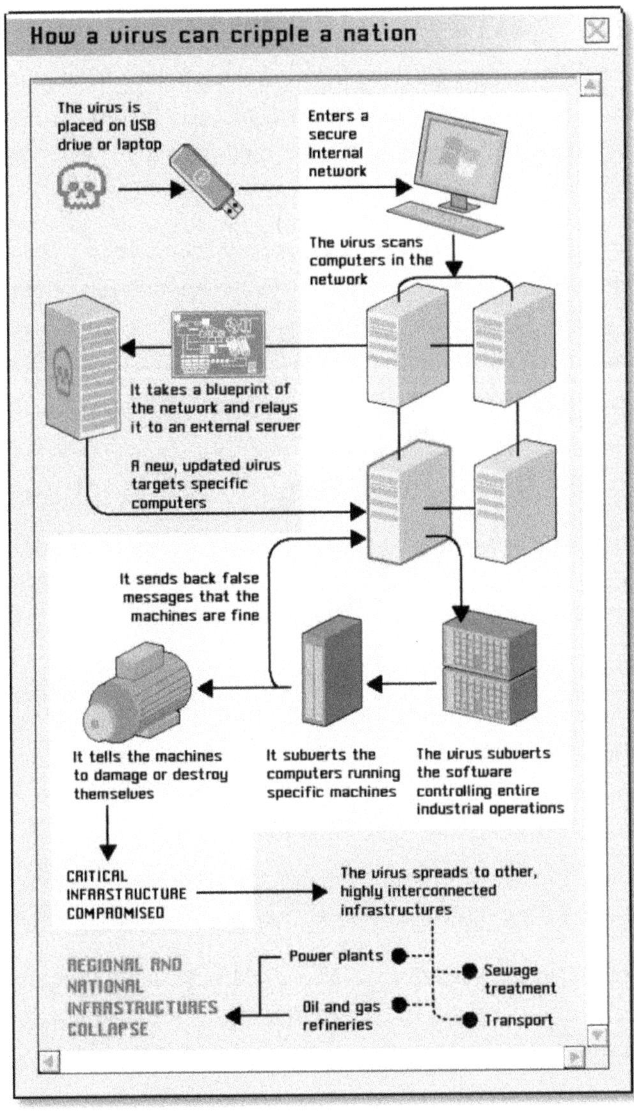

Source: https://www.nature.com/articles/474142a

Key Considerations for OT systems:

1. OT Focused Risk Assessment

Conduct a thorough OT systems risk assessment to identify and prioritize cybersecurity risks specific to your business. Evaluate both digital and physical vulnerabilities and their potential consequences.

OT being a specialized domain, calls for specialized vendors to assist you with the assessment. Don't depend on your regular IT security auditor to conduct this unless they specialize in OT as well.

2. IT-OT Integrated Security Architecture

Implement an integrated security architecture that encompasses both cyber and physical security controls, ensuring end-to-end protection of your OT systems from external threats and internal risks.

Many a times functionally interconnected IT and OT systems are responsible for various attacks exploiting this interconnect vulnerability.

3. OT Access Control and Authentication:

Implement robust access control and authentication mechanisms to restrict unauthorized access to cyber-physical systems, critical components, and functionalities.

This is crucial for keeping the OT environment safe and restrict access to authorized personnel only.

4. Encryption and Data Protection

Encrypt sensitive data transmitted and stored by OT systems to:

- prevent unauthorized interception or tampering.
- maintain data confidentiality, integrity, and authenticity throughout its lifecycle.

This may not be always possible depending on the HCIs and machineries in use but follow this rule as far as possible.

5. Resilience and Redundancy

Build resilience and redundancies into OT systems to withstand cyber-attacks, system failures, or disruptions, including redundant components, failover mechanisms.

Disaster recovery plans should govern and mitigate cyber-attacks to the best of your capabilities.

6. Continuous Monitoring and Detection

Promptly deploy real-time monitoring and detection capabilities especially for OT systems to detect and respond to anomalous behaviour or security incidents, enabling rapid containment and remediation of threats.

Note: Remember it's not only data at risk here, but an attack on an OT environment can also pose a threat to life for people working in that environment or for people using the end product.

7. Vendor and Supply Chain Security

OT environment vendors tend to be notoriously slow in patching their software bugs. Assess and manage cybersecurity risks associated with third-party vendors, suppliers, and service providers involved in the design, development, deployment, and maintenance of OT systems.

If a security control cannot be applied, then you should investigate the deployment of compensating controls which will provide a layer of security around the OT environment.

Wrap-Up

By adopting these OT specific strategies and best practices, organizations can enhance the reliability, safety, security, and resilience of their cyber-physical systems.

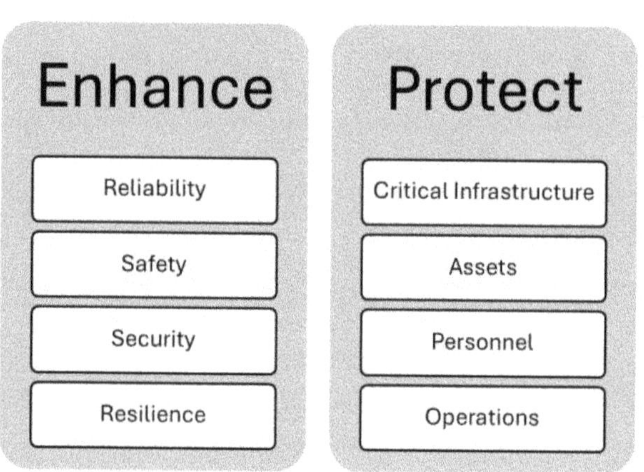

Chapter 10

We build software, anything important for us?

In today's digital age, software development is at the core of innovation and business success. Whether developing applications for internal use or delivering solutions for clients, baking security into software throughout the development lifecycle is paramount.

That's commonly known as **DevSecOps**.

This chapter explores best practices and strategies for securing software development processes, whether for in-house projects or client engagements.

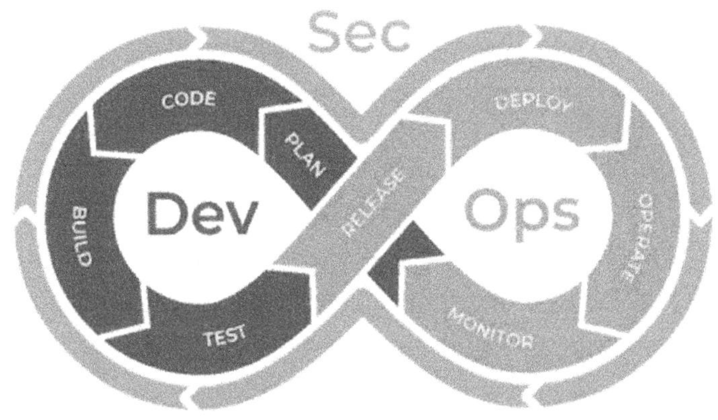

Key security considerations with software development

1. Secure Coding Practices

Developers should adopt secure coding practices, and industry standard coding guidelines which are fundamental to building resilient and secure software.

The OWASP Secure Coding Practices is a comprehensive list of guidelines to minimize the risk of common vulnerabilities in web and mobile applications such as injection flaws, cross-site scripting (XSS), and insecure data storage.

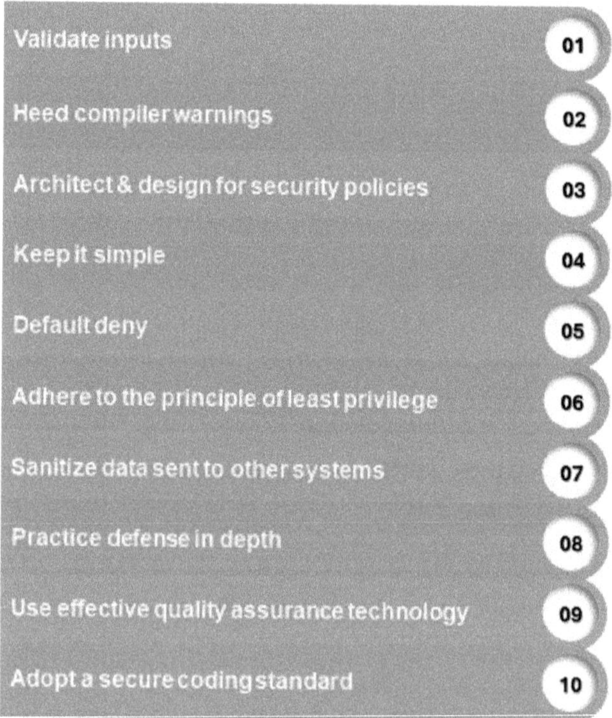

2. Security by Design

Integrating security into the software development process from the outset is essential for building secure applications.

Implement security controls and mechanisms at each stage of the development lifecycle, from requirements gathering to deployment This helps identify and mitigate security risks early, reducing the likelihood of vulnerabilities making their way into the final product.

3. Code Reviews and Static Analysis

Conduct regular code reviews and leverage static analysis tools to help identify potential security flaws and vulnerabilities in the codebase. Review code for adherence to secure coding practices and conducting automated scans for common vulnerabilities. Now developers can proactively address security issues before they manifest into serious threats.

4. Secure Development Frameworks and Libraries

Leverage secure development frameworks and libraries to expedite the development process and application architecture. Use of trusted and well-maintained frameworks and libraries helps mitigate the risk of introducing vulnerabilities through third-party dependencies.

5. Secure Configuration Management

Implement secure configuration practices for development environments, servers, and software components to reduce the attack surface, minimize exposure to security threats to bolster secure software deployments.

These practices could include to limit access privileges, disable unnecessary services, and apply security patches promptly.

6. Secure Cloud Computing

Explore best practices for securing cloud environments and data stored in the cloud, including strategies for identity and access management, encryption, and cloud security architecture.

7. Secure Deployment and DevSecOps

Incorporate security into the deployment pipeline, embracing DevSecOps principles. This enables organizations to automate security checks and enforce security controls throughout the software delivery process. Integration of security testing, vulnerability scanning, and compliance checks into the CI/CD pipeline, organizations can accelerate delivery and maintain a strong security posture.

8. Mobile Application Security

Discuss with your dev team the techniques and guidelines for secure mobile application development against common threats such as insecure data storage, improper session management, and mobile malware, etc.

Refer to OWASP Mobile Security Testing Guide as a good starting point.

9. Internet of Things (IoT) Security

Examine the unique security challenges posed by IoT devices and ecosystems, including vulnerabilities in IoT firmware, communication protocols, and physical security controls, and strategies for mitigating IoT-related risks.

Refer to the previous chapter, learnings from OT can be repurposed for IoT as well including the Purdue Reference Architecture Model.

10. Secure Software Development Training

Secure Software Development Lifecycle (SSDLC) training is essential to equip development teams with the knowledge and skills needed to build secure software from the ground up.

This training emphasizes the integration of security practices at every phase of the software development lifecycle, from planning and design to coding, testing, and maintenance.

SSDLC training fosters a culture of security empowerment, ensuring that security is not an afterthought but a fundamental component of the development process. This proactive approach not only enhances the security and reliability of software products but also helps organizations comply with regulatory requirements and protect sensitive data from cyber threats.

11. Shift LEFT strategy

If you plot software dev on a timeline, it will look like this.

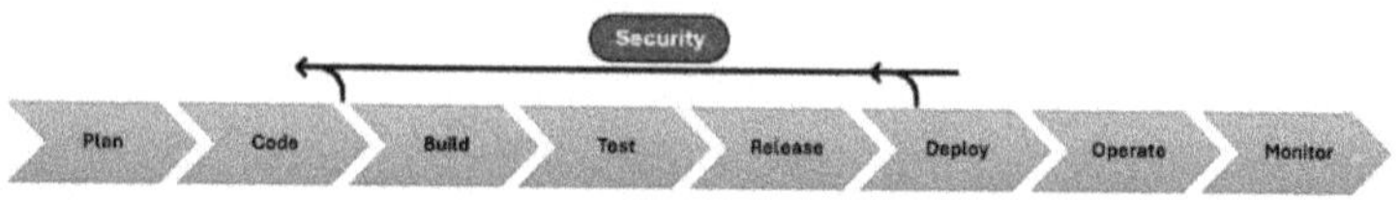

Shift left says move security leftward, before and during dev.

By shifting security activities "leftward" in the development lifecycle, organizations can identify and address security vulnerabilities and issues at the earliest stages, reducing the likelihood of costly and time-consuming security incidents later in the development lifecycle or post-deployment.

This proactive approach emphasizes collaboration between development and security teams, incorporating security requirements and considerations into the design and coding phases, conducting static code analysis, and implementing automated security testing tools.

12. Regulatory Compliance and Data Privacy

Examine the landscape of global regulatory frameworks and data privacy laws, such as GDPR, CCPA, and HIPAA, and provide guidance on achieving compliance, managing data privacy risks, and responding to regulatory requirements.

Wrap-Up

By adhering to these best practices and integrating security into every aspect of the software development lifecycle, organizations can build resilient and secure software that meets the needs of internal stakeholders and clients alike.

Prioritizing security in software development not only mitigates risks and protects sensitive data but also enhances trust, credibility, and long-term success in an increasingly digital world.

Chapter 11

Where can I contribute?

Your office is where:

- Decisions are made
- Strategies are crafted
- Visions are brought to life

As a business leader, you're not just a figurehead – you're a steward of your organization's future, entrusted with the responsibility of guiding it through the choppy waters of the business world. But when it comes to cybersecurity, where exactly do you fit in?

As the highest level of oversight, board members play a pivotal role in ensuring effective cybersecurity practices within their organizations. By actively engaging in cybersecurity policy discussions and decision-making processes, board members can help establish a culture of security and help prepare an organization to mitigate cyber-attacks.

1. Board & Senior Management Responsibilities

Setting the Tone at the Top

- Champion a culture of cybersecurity awareness and accountability
- Prioritize cybersecurity as a strategic priority
- Lead by example in adhering to industry best practices and policies.

Governance and Oversight

- Provide strategic direction and oversight of cybersecurity efforts
- Establish clear roles, responsibilities
- Create reporting mechanisms for cybersecurity governance and risk management

Risk Management and Compliance

- Assess and prioritize cybersecurity risks
- Align with the organization's overall risk appetite and regulatory requirements
- Oversee the implementation of risk mitigation strategies and compliance initiatives

Cybersecurity Strategy and Investments

- Review and approve the organization's cybersecurity strategy, budget, and investments
- Allocate resources effectively to address key cybersecurity risks and priorities

Executive Leadership Support

Provide guidance and support to executive leadership, including the Chief Information Security Officer (CISO) or equivalent, in implementing cybersecurity initiatives and addressing emerging threats and challenges.

Stakeholder Engagement

Engage with key stakeholders, including shareholders, customers, regulators, and industry peers, on cybersecurity matters, fostering transparency, trust, and collaboration in addressing shared cybersecurity risks and concerns.

Incident Handling and Crisis Management

Oversee the organization's cybersecurity incident response and crisis management:

- Detection Readiness: Mean Time To Detect (MTTD)
- Response Effectiveness: Mean Time To Acknowledge (MTTA)
- Recovery abilities: Mean Time To Recover (MTTR)

in a timely and effective manner.

Board Education and Training

Stay informed about emerging cybersecurity trends, threats, and best practices through ongoing education and training opportunities, and leverage your knowledge and expertise to guide informed decision-making and governance.

Continuous Improvement

Evaluate the effectiveness of cybersecurity efforts and governance practices through:

- Regular assessments
- Audits and reviews
- Drive continuous improvement initiatives

to enhance the organization's cyber resilience and readiness.

Wrap-Up

Remember, cybersecurity is not just a technology issue – it's a business imperative that requires:

- Leadership
- Vision
- Commitment

to protect your organization's most valuable assets and secure its future.

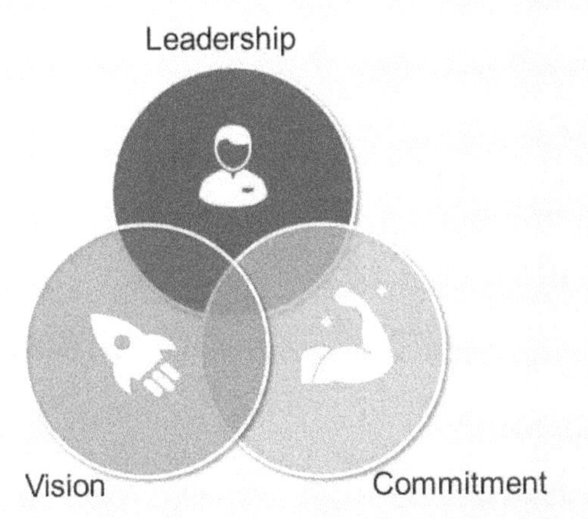

Chapter 12

What if there is a security incident?

Ah, the unexpected twists and turns of the digital world – where even the best-laid plans can sometimes go awry. In the realm of cybersecurity, preparation is the name of the game.

As a business leader, tasked with steering your organization through the choppy waters of cyber threats and incidents, having a robust incident response plan in place is not just a luxury – it's a necessity.

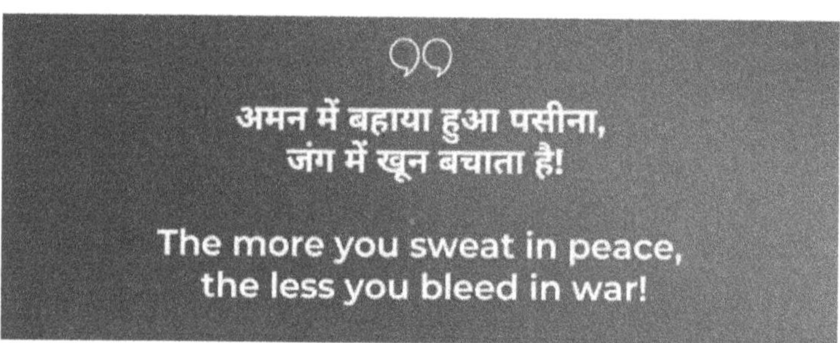

1. Incident Response Planning

Preparation and Readiness

- Establish a formalized incident response team and plan
- Outline roles, responsibilities, and procedures for detecting, assessing, and responding to cybersecurity incidents in a timely and effective manner.

Risk Assessment and Incident Classification

- Conduct regular risk assessments to identify potential cybersecurity threats and vulnerabilities
- Develop a classification scheme to categorize incidents based on their severity, impact, and urgency.

Incident Detection and Reporting

- Implement monitoring and detection capabilities to identify and alert on suspicious activities or security events
- Establish clear channels and protocols for reporting incidents to the incident response team and relevant stakeholders.

Response and Containment

Define response procedures and escalation paths for containing and mitigating the impact of cybersecurity incidents, including:

- Isolating affected systems
- Preserving evidence
- Restoring normal operations as quickly as possible

Communication and Coordination

Establish communication protocols and channels for coordinating incident response efforts internally and externally, including notifying executive leadership, legal counsel, regulatory authorities, and other stakeholders as required.

Forensics and Investigation

- Conduct post-incident analysis and forensic investigations to determine the root cause of incidents
- Identify lessons learned
- Implement corrective actions to prevent future recurrences.

Documentation and Reporting

- Document all aspects of incident response activities, including incident details, response actions taken, and lessons learned
- Prepare post-incident reports for review by executive leadership and regulatory authorities

Training and Exercises

- Provide regular training and tabletop exercises for incident response team members and stakeholders to rehearse response procedures
- Test communication channels
- Validate incident response plan effectiveness

Continuous Improvement

Review and update the incident response plan regularly based on lessons from:

- Real-world incidents
- Changes in the threat landscape
- Emerging best practices

ensuring that it remains current, effective, and aligned with the organization's evolving needs and priorities.

2. Your Role in Incident Response Planning

Governance and Oversight

- Provide strategic direction and oversight of incident response planning efforts
- Align organization's incident response capabilities with business objectives, risk appetite, and regulatory requirements.

Resource Allocation

- Allocate resources, including budget, personnel, and technology, to support incident response planning and implementation activities
- Ensure that the organization has the necessary tools and capabilities to detect, respond to, and recover from cybersecurity incidents.

Executive Leadership Support

- Champion incident response planning efforts within the organization
- Advocate for the importance of preparedness and resilience in addressing cybersecurity risks
- Ensure executive buy-in and support for incident response initiatives

Stakeholder Engagement

- Engage with key stakeholders, including executive leadership, legal counsel, IT & security teams, and external partners
- Foster collaboration and coordination in incident response planning and execution
- Ensuring that all parties are informed and aligned in their roles and responsibilities.

Training and Education

- Participate in incident response planning through ongoing education and training opportunities
- Stay informed about emerging threats, trends, and best practices
- Leverage knowledge and expertise to make informed decisions for governance

Evaluation and Improvement

- Monitor and evaluate the effectiveness of incident response planning efforts through regular assessments, reviews, and exercises
- Drive continuous improvement initiatives to enhance the organization's incident response capabilities and readiness to address cybersecurity incidents

Wrap-Up

By actively engaging in incident response planning and governance, leadership can play a crucial role in ensuring that their organizations are prepared, resilient, and ready to respond effectively. This preparedness will minimize attack impact and safeguard company operations, reputation, and stakeholders' trust.

Remember, in the face of uncertainty and adversity, preparation is the key to resilience.

3. Handling investigation and breaches

Sh!t happens, manage it 😊

Cyber incidents can happen and disrupt operations, compromise sensitive data, and damage reputation. Effectively managing and investigating incidents is paramount to minimizing their impact and restoring normalcy.

Initial Triage

Maintain Evidence

Regulatory Reporting

Avoid Ambulance Chasers

Threat Intelligence

Media Management

Initial Triage:

- Promptly identify and prioritize incidents based on severity, impact, and potential risks to the organization.
- Establish an incident response team comprising representatives from IT, security, legal, and communications departments to coordinate response efforts.
- Gather initial information about the incident, including the nature of the threat, affected systems or assets, and potential indicators of compromise.

- Report to CERT-India and inform them about the attack with 6-8 hours of you knowing about the attack.

Maintain Evidence:

- Preserve and document evidence related to the incident to support investigation and potential legal proceedings.
- Implement forensic techniques to capture volatile data, such as memory dumps and network traffic logs.
- Adhere to chain of custody procedures to maintain the integrity of evidence and ensure its admissibility in court, if necessary.

Regulatory Reporting:

- Determine if the incident triggers mandatory reporting obligations under relevant regulations, such as CERT in, GDPR, HIPAA, or PCI DSS.
- Comply with reporting requirements by notifying regulatory authorities, affected individuals, and other stakeholders in a timely manner.
- Collaborate with legal counsel to navigate regulatory obligations and mitigate legal risks associated with non-compliance.

Avoiding Ambulance Chasers:

- Beware of opportunistic individuals or entities seeking to capitalize on incidents for personal gain or malicious intent.
- Vet third-party service providers, such as forensic investigators or legal firms, to ensure credibility, competence, and ethical conduct.

- Implement measures to protect sensitive information and mitigate the risk of extortion, blackmail, or further exploitation by threat actors.

Collaborate & Communicate:

- Maintain open lines of communication with internal stakeholders, including executives, employees, and board members, to provide timely updates and address concerns.
- Collaborate with external partners, such as law enforcement agencies, industry peers, and cybersecurity experts, to share threat intelligence and leverage collective expertise in incident response.

Media Management:

- Develop a proactive media strategy to manage public perception and protect the organization's reputation during and after an incident.
- Designate a spokesperson or communications team to handle media inquiries and disseminate accurate information to external stakeholders.
- Balance transparency with confidentiality, disclosing only essential details to maintain trust while safeguarding sensitive information.

Wrap-Up

Many organizations neglect to invest time and money in developing incident response strategies. When an incident does occur, it is critical that all focus is on recovering from the incident. This is possible when everyone knows their specific roles and responsibilities.

Incident response should operate like a well-oiled machine so that the organization can recover from the attack in minimal time with minimal loss. This is possible via incident response and recovery drills.

Identifying your risk areas ahead of time will prepare you better. All risks cannot be mitigated simultaneously for several reasons. Hence knowing your open risks can prepare you better.

Ensuring that the correct information flows at the right time to the right people via the right channels is of paramount importance. This prevents misinformation and unnecessary panic amongst your stakeholders.

Finally, as a business leader remember that the buck stops with you, and it would be prudent to stand steadfast with your team during an incident. Hosting a blame game will only prolong the recovery process.

4. Handling external party reporting directly

Many times, you'll receive emails from external parties referring to a bug on your website. This is a common occurrence, and it's essential to handle these reports effectively.

BugBounty (aka RVDP)

BugBounty Program also known as Responsible Vulnerability Disclosure Programs (RVDPs) plays a pivotal role in cybersecurity by providing a structured framework for security researchers and ethical hackers to responsibly report security vulnerabilities they discover in software and systems.

Few RVDP pages listed below for your reference

Company	RVDP Link
META	https://bugbounty.meta.com/
Google	https://bughunters.google.com/
Apple	https://security.apple.com/bounty/

Reporting a Vulnerability

Serious researchers will use email or other official channels to reach out to your company and secretly report a vulnerability to get it fixed.

RVDP programs outline guidelines and procedures for reporting vulnerabilities to organizations, allowing them to assess, triage, and remediate the reported issues promptly.

Encourage this culture as it benefits both, the researchers, and the organization.

> **CAUTION:** RVDP involves officially announcing that your organization is ready for external researchers to identify issues in their infrastructure. This can also invite attackers to identify issues for malicious purposes such as data exfiltration, malware propagation, ransomware etc.

To avoid this, ensure you have reached a decent level of security maturity in your infrastructure.

Rewards

In return for responsibly disclosing vulnerabilities, many companies offer rewards or bug bounties to security researchers as a token of appreciation for their efforts in improving security.

These rewards can vary in value depending on the severity of the reported vulnerability and the organization's policies, ranging from monetary compensation to recognition in hall of fame lists or swag items.

Main intention here is resolving the bug and securing the software. Any reward associated is deemed an extra benefit.

Companies do reward serious findings for. e.g., Google pays $1,337 or $31,337 based on severity and Meta paid over $2 million in bounties and received 10,000 reports.

Severity	Median	Competitive	Top
Low	$100 USD	$300 USD	$500 USD
Medium	$300 USD	$500 USD	$750 USD
High	$500 USD	$750 USD	$1,000 USD
Critical	$1,000 USD and up	$1,500 USD and up	$2,000 USD and up

Here are tentative numbers to give you an idea.

As a result, RVDPs:

- Fosters collaboration between security researchers and organizations
- Incentivizes proactive security research
- Contributes to the overall resilience of digital ecosystems

If you want to leverage power of RVDP in securing your posture, you can either run this program yourself or outsource it to a reputed firm who will operate the BugBounty on your behalf.

BegBounty (Yes Beg, not BugBounty)

While bug bounty programs incentivize ethical security researchers to responsibly disclose vulnerabilities, there is also a phenomenon known as "BegBounty," where individuals may attempt to exploit the system by resorting to begging for rewards, often without providing substantial or legitimate findings.

In most cases, these individuals exaggerate the severity of reported issues or conceal critical details to elicit a reward from organizations. BegBounty causes an influx of low-quality or non-actionable reports, making it difficult to prioritize and address genuine security vulnerabilities effectively.

Do not encourage this at all.

To mitigate the impact of BegBounty, organizations must establish clear guidelines and criteria for evaluating bug reports, conduct thorough assessments to validate reported vulnerabilities, and maintain transparency and integrity in their reward and recognition processes.

Additionally, fostering a culture of ethical behaviour and accountability within the security research community can help deter individuals from engaging in "BegBounty" activities and uphold the integrity of "BugBounty" programs.

Chapter 13

Still why should I do it?

"Still... should I really be bothered so much about security?"

"It's expensive, time-consuming; frankly, a headache I don't want"

Ah, the familiar refrain of many a weary board director faced with the daunting task of navigating the labyrinthine world of cybersecurity.

Let's examine why cybersecurity – driven partly by regulatory requirements – is not a necessary evil but a crucial aspect of protecting your organization's interests and ensuring its long-term success.

These regulatory and non-regulatory frameworks also provide a good guiding north star to keep the security program on a sensible track.

Here are a few reasons why companies do not implement cyber security controls:

"We're a small company, surely, they won't bother coming after us,"

"We've been doing just fine without all these regulations so far,"

The reality is that regulatory compliance is not just about avoiding hefty fines and legal headaches (although that's certainly a compelling reason in itself).

It's about safeguarding your organization's reputation, maintaining customer trust, and demonstrating your commitment to ethical and responsible business practices in an increasingly regulated and scrutinized world.

The Elephant in the room

Now, let's address the elephant in the room – the sheer volume and complexity of regulatory requirements can indeed be overwhelming, especially for organizations operating in multiple geographies, jurisdictions, or industries.

From data privacy and protection laws like the GDPR in Europe to healthcare regulations like HIPAA in the United States and regulations like CERT-In / IRDA / RBI guidelines in India, the regulatory landscape is a veritable minefield of requirements, standards, and mandates waiting to trip up the unprepared.

By understanding the key regulations applicable to your industry, geography, and business operations, you can take proactive steps to meet compliance requirements and remain resilient in the face of regulatory scrutiny and enforcement actions.

So, without further ado, let's explore some of the most prominent regulatory compliance frameworks and requirements shaping the global business landscape today.

1. Global Regulatory Compliance Frameworks

These are some of the regulatory compliances that your organisation may have to follow to operate in a particular industry or geography. Your CISO or Virtual CISO is the best person to guide you on what may be applicable to your organization.

GDPR (General Data Protection Regulation)

Applicable to organizations that process the personal data of EU residents, GDPR imposes strict requirements for data protection, privacy, and consent, with hefty fines for non-compliance.

CPRA (California Privacy Rights Act)

Provides California residents with enhanced privacy rights and imposes obligations on businesses to disclose their data practices, respond to consumer requests, and implement data protection measures.

HIPAA (Health Insurance Portability and Accountability Act)

Governs the protection and security of healthcare information in the United States, requiring healthcare providers, insurers, and other covered entities to safeguard patient data and privacy.

PCI-DSS (Payment Card Industry Data Security Standard)

Applies to organizations that handle credit card payments, requiring them to implement security controls and measures to protect cardholder data from breaches and fraud. With time, the coverage has increased beyond the scope of only card payments. Now all financial systems are covered by PCI.

MAS Singapore (Monetary Authority of Singapore) Guidelines

Issued by the Monetary Authority of Singapore, these guidelines provide regulatory requirements and best practices for financial institutions in Singapore to enhance their cybersecurity resilience and compliance with industry standards.

NESA UAE (National Electronic Security Authority) Guidelines

NESA stands for National Electronic Security Authority and is a government institution that aims to provide strict guidelines to organizations for keeping their information security capabilities in line with the highest standards to avoid cybersecurity threats.

2. Indian Regulatory Compliance Frameworks

RBI (Reserve Bank of India) Guidelines

Regulates banking and financial services in India, including requirements for cybersecurity, data protection, and customer information security.

RBI Guidelines on Cyber Security framework primarily focuses on the following three areas:

- Cyber Security and Resilience
- Cyber Security Operations Centre (C-SOC)
- Cyber Security Incident Reporting (CSIR)

Banks need to assess their Cyber Security preparedness under the active guidance and oversight of the IT Sub Committee of the Board or the Bank's Board directly.

IRDAI (Insurance Regulatory and Development Authority of India) Guidelines

These guidelines outline cybersecurity requirements and standards for insurance companies operating in India, aiming to enhance data protection, risk management, and incident response capabilities within the insurance sector.

SEBI (Securities and Exchange Board of India) Guidelines

SEBI issues guidelines and regulations related to cybersecurity and information security practices for entities operating in the securities market in India, aiming to safeguard investor interests, market integrity, and financial stability.

DPDP (Digital Personal Data Protection Act)

Introduces comprehensive data protection and privacy regulations for the processing of personal data in India, imposing obligations on organizations to protect individuals' privacy rights and data subjects' rights.

We authored an eBook on 10th Aug 2023 (a day before president signed the bill to be an act) titled "Navigating The Digital Personal Data Protection Bill of India – 2023".

The same can be accessed at

https://www.rohit11.com/2023/08/10/new-ebook-navigating-the-digital-personal-data-protection-bill-of-india-2023/

CERT-IN Guidelines

Offers cybersecurity guidelines and best practices issued by CERT-IN to enhance organizational security posture, covering areas such as risk management, incident response, and secure coding practices.

CERT-In issued a much needed and welcome set of directives aimed at enhancing the security profile of organisations operating within the Indian jurisdiction.

We authored a free eBook to demystify the directive which can be accessed at

https://www.rohit11.com/2022/06/12/demystifying-cert-in-directives-dated-28th-april-2022/

3. Non-Regulatory Security Frameworks

While these may not be mandatory for your business but can help channelise the security program well and at times may be asked by your clients. Ask your Virtual CISO for the same.

ISO 27001

An international standard for information security management systems (ISMS), providing a framework for organizations to establish, implement, maintain, and continually improve their information security posture.

This is one of the most popular frameworks used by many organizations to establish industry security practices and discipline in the organization.

Service Organization Control (SOC) 2

The primary purpose of a SOC2 framework is required by third party providers which process and store client data and oversee that they do so in a secure manner.

SOC2 is centred around the following 5 principles: Security, Availability, Integrity, Confidentiality, and Privacy.

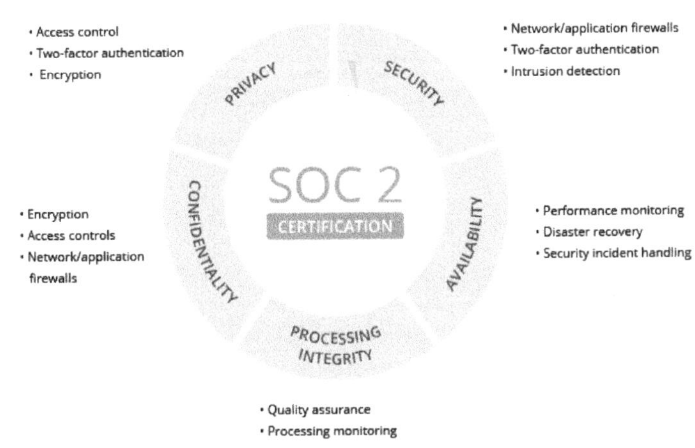

To obtain a SOC2 certificate, an external independent auditor must verify presence of relevant controls and if their correct configurations are deployed.

Health Information Trust Alliance (HITRUST)

A framework for healthcare specific organizations to assess and manage cybersecurity risks and compliance with industry-specific regulations and standards.

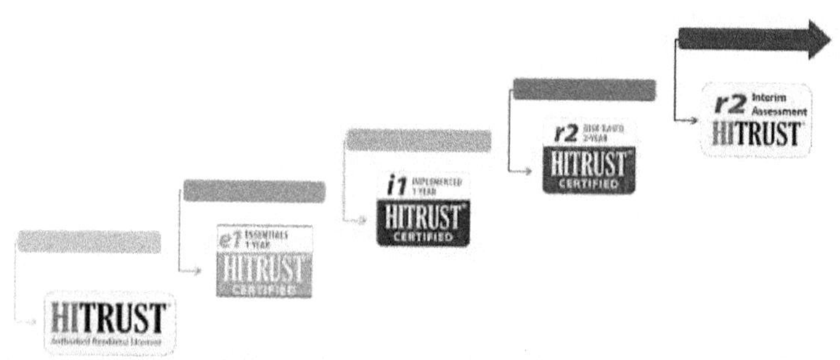

HITRUST CSF framework is used as a guideline if your organization works in the healthcare domain and collects, stores, and/or processes health care information.

NIST Cybersecurity Framework (CSF)

Provides a flexible framework for managing cybersecurity risk, developed by NIST, encompassing five core functions: Identify, Protect, Detect, Respond, and Recover.

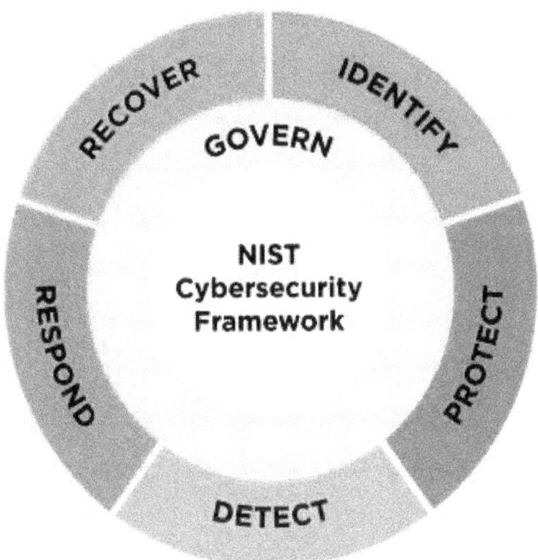

Developed by National Institute of Standards and Technology and currently in its 2nd version, NIST CSF is one of the most widely used and accepted frameworks. Many enterprises derive their security roadmap from this framework.

In fact, many countries design their cyber security initiatives, and local regulatory requirements based on NIST CSF.

MITRE ATT&CK and D3FEND

MITRE has released 2 global frameworks (ATT&CK and D3FEND).

ATT&CK framework comprises adversary techniques and tactics.

D3FEND framework comprises mitigation techniques for cyber threats.

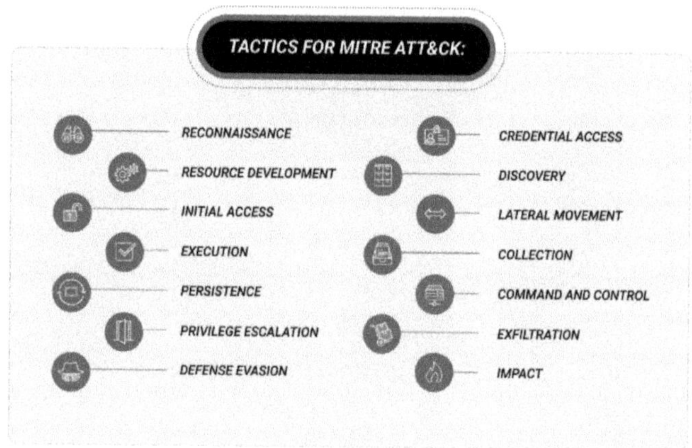

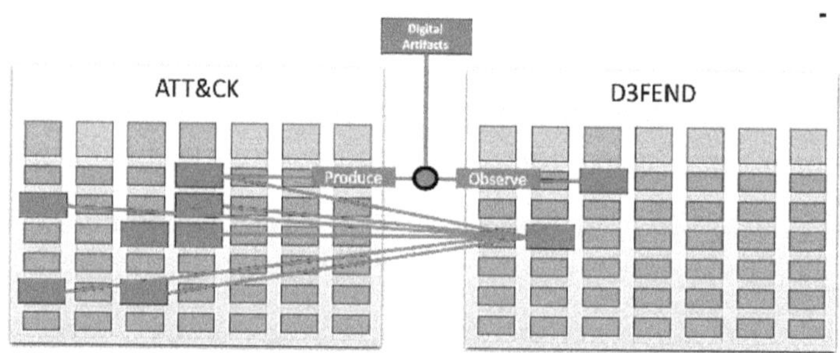

The Cyber Kill Chain

Developed by Lockheed Martin, the Cyber Kill Chain framework is part of the Intelligence Driven Defence model for identification and prevention of cyber intrusions activity.

The model identifies the steps adversaries must complete to achieve their objective. The seven steps of the Cyber Kill Chain® enhance visibility into an attack and enriches an analyst's understanding of an adversary's tactics, techniques, and procedures.

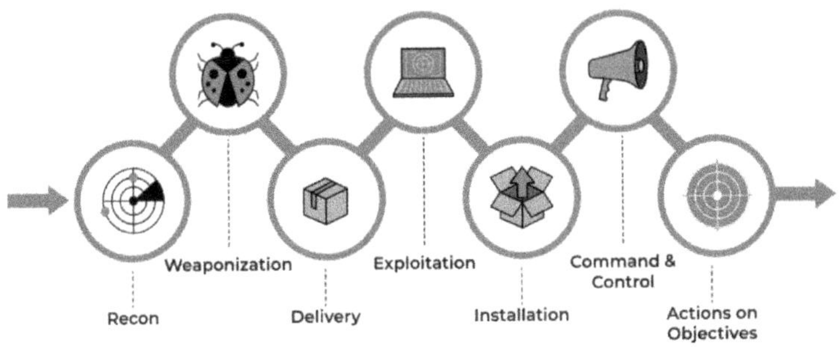

Wrap-Up

These are just a few examples of the myriad regulatory compliance frameworks and requirements that business leaders must navigate to meet legal requirements & compliance obligations, mitigate risks, and maintain stakeholder trust in an increasingly regulated and interconnected world.

> Benefits of upholding ethical and responsible business practices far outweigh the costs of non-compliance.

If in doubt, speak to your CISO and/or Virtual CISO.

Chapter 14

How do I build a cyber-aware culture?

In the fast-paced world of cybersecurity, technology alone cannot guarantee protection against evolving threats – it's the human element that often proves to be both the weakest link and the strongest defence.

As a board director, fostering a cyber-aware culture within your organization is not just a lofty goal – it's a strategic imperative that can mean the difference between resilience and vulnerability in the face of cyber threats.

1. Leadership Commitment

Demonstrate visible and vocal support for cybersecurity awareness and education initiatives from executive leadership and the board, setting the tone at the top and signalling the organization's commitment to cyber resilience.

Education and Training

Provide regular cybersecurity awareness training and educational programs for employees at all levels, covering topics such as phishing awareness, password security, data protection, and incident reporting procedures.

Tailored Content and Delivery

Develop customized training materials and delivery methods that resonate with different audiences and job roles within the organization, ensuring relevance and engagement in cybersecurity awareness initiatives.

Continuous Reinforcement

Reinforce cybersecurity awareness messages and best practices through ongoing communication channels, including email reminders, intranet articles, posters, and interactive quizzes, to keep cybersecurity top of mind for employees.

Simulation Exercises

Conduct simulated phishing exercises and tabletop simulations to test employees' awareness and response to phishing attacks, data breaches, and other cybersecurity incidents, providing hands-on experience in recognizing and mitigating cyber threats.

Positive Reinforcement

Recognize and reward employees who demonstrate good cybersecurity practices and behaviours, fostering a culture of accountability and positive reinforcement for cyber-aware actions.

Open Communication Channels

Encourage open communication and feedback channels for employees to report security incidents, ask questions, and share concerns about cybersecurity, creating a supportive and collaborative environment for addressing cybersecurity challenges.

Leading by Example

Lead by example in practicing good cybersecurity hygiene and behaviours, such as using strong passwords, following security policies, and promptly reporting suspicious activities or security incidents, inspiring others to follow suit.

Metrics and Measurement

Establish metrics and key performance indicators (KPIs) to measure the effectiveness of cybersecurity awareness initiatives, such as phishing click rates, incident reporting rates, and employee feedback scores, and use this data to refine and improve awareness programs over time.

Integration with Business Processes

Integrate cybersecurity awareness and education into existing business processes and workflows, embedding cybersecurity considerations into employee onboarding, training programs, performance evaluations, and corporate culture initiatives.

2. Your Role in Building a Cyber-Aware Culture

Championing Cybersecurity Awareness: Advocate for the importance of cybersecurity awareness and education initiatives within the organization, leveraging your influence and credibility to garner support from executive leadership, management, and employees.

Strategic Direction

Allocating Resources

Leading by Example

Monitoring and Evaluation

Continuous Improvement

Providing Strategic Direction

Provide strategic direction and oversight for cybersecurity awareness programs, ensuring alignment with organizational goals, priorities, and risk management objectives.

Allocating Resources

Allocate resources, including budget, personnel, and technology, to support cybersecurity awareness and education initiatives, ensuring adequate funding and support for ongoing initiatives and initiatives.

Leading by Example

Lead by example in demonstrating good cybersecurity practices and behaviours, serving as a role model and inspiration for employees to adopt cyber-aware habits and behaviours in their daily activities.

Monitoring and Evaluation

Monitor the effectiveness of cybersecurity awareness programs through regular assessments, feedback mechanisms, and performance metrics, and use this data to identify areas for improvement and optimization.

Continuous Improvement

Drive continuous improvement and innovation in cybersecurity awareness and education initiatives, staying abreast of emerging trends, best practices, and technologies to enhance the organization's cyber resilience and readiness.

Wrap-Up

By championing cybersecurity awareness and education initiatives, business leaders can cultivate a culture where cybersecurity is not just a box to tick but a shared responsibility and core business value.

In this culture of awareness, cybersecurity becomes ingrained in the organization's DNA, creating a resilient and adaptive environment where everyone plays a role in protecting the organization's digital assets and reputation.

Chapter 15

How to keep myself updated?

In the ever-evolving landscape of cybersecurity, staying informed is not just a luxury – it's a necessity. As a board director entrusted with safeguarding your organization's interests in the digital realm, keeping yourself updated to make informed decisions and effectively navigate the complexities of the cyber landscape.

1. In person

Industry Conferences and Events

Attend renowned cybersecurity conferences and events such as

- Black Hat (Las Vegas, London, Singapore, MEA)
- DEF CON (Las Vegas)
- RSA Conference (San Francisco)
- Gartner Security & Risk Management Summit (Mumbai and Globally)
- DSCI AISS (Delhi NCR, India)
- FIRST Annual Conference (Global locations)
- Hack In The Box (Asia / Middle East / Europe)
- Nullcon (India, EU)
- c0c0n (India)
- OneConference (Netherlands)

to gain insights into emerging threats, innovative technologies, and best practices from industry experts and thought leaders.

Regional and Local Conferences

Exposing your team to participate in regional and local cybersecurity conferences and events tailored to your geographic location or industry sector provides them opportunities to network with peers, share experiences, and learn about region-specific security challenges and solutions.

This exposure is invaluable as it ingrains the importance of cyber security within your teams.

To further enforce, host a session in your office premises where the team presents a gist of the event as a deliverable.

The best way to find local community conferences is:

https://infosec-conferences.com/

Local Meetups and Community Events

Participate in local cybersecurity meetups, workshops, and community events organized by industry groups, academic institutions, and cybersecurity startups to network with professionals, share experiences, and learn from local experts.

Identify local community events like BSides etc and encourage your teams to attend them. Sometimes attending smaller conferences could be more beneficial due to a more personal environment.

2. Online

Cybersecurity Blogs and Websites

Follow reputable cybersecurity blogs and websites, to stay updated on the latest cybersecurity news, analysis, research findings, and expert opinions.

Here are a few for your reference:

- **Krebs on Security** krebsonsecurity.com
- **Schneier on Security** schneier.com
- **The Hacker News** thehackernews.com
- **Security Affairs** securityaffairs.com
- **The 420** the420.in
- **SC Magazine** scmagazine.com

Podcasts and Webinars

Subscribe to cybersecurity podcasts and webinars featuring discussions, interviews, and insights from cybersecurity professionals, researchers, and thought leaders. They offer convenient and accessible ways to stay informed while on the go.

Some good ones to follow are:

- CyberWire Daily
- N2K Hacking Human
- Smashing Security
- SANS ISC StormCast
- Darknet Diaries

Social Media and Online Communities

Join cybersecurity focused social media groups, forums, and online communities on platforms like LinkedIn, Twitter, and Reddit to engage with like-minded professionals, share knowledge, and discuss current cybersecurity topics and trends.

If you are on twitter / X, we suggest you follow

- Rohit Srivastwa (@rohit11)
- Aalok Karnik (@aalok_the_k)

Obviously, we'll start by our names, but other good twitter/X accounts to follow includes:
- The Hacker News (@thehackernews)
- Cyber Dost (@Cyberdost)
- Dave Kennedy (@HackingDave)
- Graham Cluley (@gcluley)
- Jason Haddix (@Jhaddix)
- Rachel Tobac (@RachelTobac)
- Robert M. Lee (@RobertMLee)
- Troy Hunt (@troyhunt)

Professional Associations and Networks

Encourage your team to become a member of professional cybersecurity associations and networks, such as ISACA, (ISC)^2, and the Information Systems Security Association (ISSA), to access exclusive resources, events, and networking opportunities for professional development.

Thought Leadership Platforms

Explore thought leadership platforms and resources offered by cybersecurity organizations, consulting firms, and research institutes, such as SANS Institute, MITRE ATT&CK, and Cybersecurity and Infrastructure Security Agency (CISA), Gartner, to access whitepapers, reports, and insights on cybersecurity trends and challenges.

Training and Certification Programs

Enrol in cybersecurity training and certification programs to expand your knowledge and skills in specific areas of cybersecurity, such as ethical hacking, incident response, and cloud security, and stay updated on industry best practices and standards.

These resources can help you equip yourself and your team with the latest happenings, knowledge, insights, and connections needed to effectively fulfil your responsibilities to strengthen the resilience and success of your organization in the digital age.

Chapter 16

How can I get attacked?

An **attack vector** is the method or combination of methods that cybercriminals use to breach or infiltrate a victim's network.

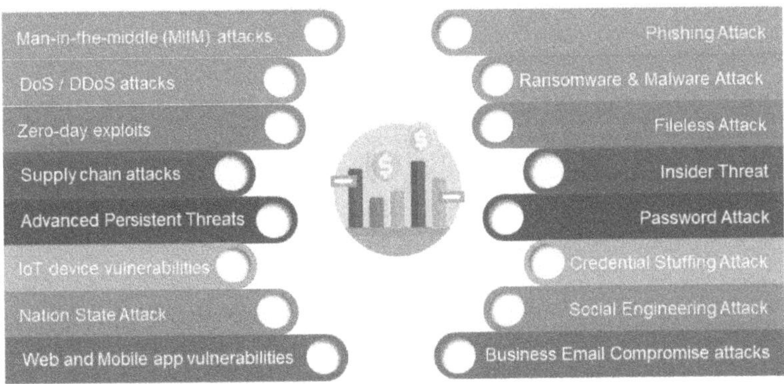

Attack surfaces can be categorized into three basic types:

Digital attack surface: comprising the entire network and software environment of an organization (applications, code, ports, ingress & egress points).

Physical attack surface: infrastructure like user endpoints, mobile devices, servers, access gates, telco infrastructure, electrical feeds.

Social engineering attack surface: exploiting the human mind, via phishing, and other manipulative techniques.

Here are some common attack vectors explained.

1. Phishing attacks

Scenario: Imagine receiving an email/SMS which appears to be from your bank, asking you to urgently update your account information by clicking on a link provided in the email/SMS. The email might look legitimate, with the bank's logo and branding, and it might even address you by name.

However, if you were to click on that link and enter your personal or financial details, you could unknowingly be handing over sensitive information to cybercriminals.

Modus Operandi: These emails are designed to trick you into divulging confidential information or downloading malicious software onto your computer.

Cybercriminals often use various tactics to make their phishing emails appear genuine, such as creating fake websites that closely resemble legitimate ones or spoofing email addresses to make them look like they're coming from a trusted source.

This can come via email, SMS, QR code, voice call, WhatsApp message or any other such channel.

Impact: Phishing attacks can have grave consequences for individuals and organizations, ranging from financial loss and identity theft to data breaches and reputational damage.

It's smart and crucial to be vigilant and sceptical of unsolicited emails, especially those requesting sensitive information or urging immediate action.

Solution:

A solution to phishing attacks involves a combination of technological measures, user education, and organizational policies:

Email Filtering	Implement robust email filtering solutions to detect and block phishing emails before they reach users' inboxes.
Employee Training	Conduct regular phishing awareness training for employees to recognize and report phishing attempts.
Multi-Factor Authentication (MFA)	Enforce MFA for accessing sensitive systems and data to prevent unauthorized access even if credentials are compromised.
Web Filtering	Use web filtering tools to block access to known phishing websites and malicious domains.
Security Software	Deploy and regularly update anti-malware and anti-phishing software to detect and block malicious URLs and attachments.
Strong Password Policies	Enforce strong password policies and regular password changes to reduce the risk of credential theft.
User Awareness	Continuously educate users about the latest phishing techniques and encourage them to be vigilant when interacting with emails, links, and attachments.

2. Malware / Ransomware infections

Scenario: Imagine sitting at your office computer, going about your daily tasks, when suddenly a pop-up appears on your screen claiming that all your important files have been encrypted and the only way to get them back is by paying a hefty sum of money. This is what we call ransomware, a type of malware infection.

Modus Operandi: Ransomware sneaks into your computer system through various means, like malicious email attachments or compromised websites.

Once it's in, it starts encrypting your files, essentially locking them away and making them inaccessible to you. Then, it demands a ransom, usually in the form of cryptocurrency, in exchange for the decryption key needed to unlock your files.

Impact: The impact of ransomware can be devastating for businesses, causing not only financial losses from the ransom payments but also operational disruptions, data loss, and reputational harm. It's like a digital hijacking of your valuable information, holding it hostage until you meet the cybercriminals' demands.

Solution:

Understanding the threat of ransomware is crucial for protecting your company's assets and reputation. Implementing robust cybersecurity measures, such as regular software updates, employee training, and data backups, can help mitigate the risk of falling victim to such malicious attacks.

3. Fileless attacks

Scenario: Think of it as a burglar using the tools already present in your home, such as kitchen utensils or household appliances, to carry out their theft without leaving behind any physical evidence of their presence.

Modus Operandi: In a fileless attack, instead of relying on traditional malware that installs files onto a victim's system, cybercriminals exploit existing legitimate programs or system tools to carry out their malicious activities directly from memory.

This technique allows attackers to evade detection by traditional antivirus software and security measures that typically scan for and block malicious files.

Impact: Fileless attacks often leverage vulnerabilities in operating systems or applications to inject malicious code into legitimate processes, allowing attackers to execute commands, steal sensitive information, or carry out other malicious activities without leaving behind any files on the victim's system.

Solution:

Deploying advanced endpoint detection and response (EDR) solutions capable of detecting and mitigating fileless threats in real-time, as well as implementing robust security practices such as regular software updates, user training on recognizing suspicious behaviour, and proactive monitoring of network activity for signs of compromise.

4. Insider threats

Scenario: You're at a company meeting, surrounded by colleagues you've known for years, when suddenly you realize that one of them has been secretly working against the company's interests. This is what we call an insider attack.

Modus Operandi: An insider attack occurs when someone within the organization, such as an employee, contractor, or trusted partner, deliberately compromises the company's security for personal gain or malicious intent. This could involve stealing sensitive information, sabotaging systems, or leaking confidential data to external parties.

Unlike external cyber threats, insider attacks can be particularly challenging to detect because the perpetrator often has legitimate access to the company's systems and information. They may exploit their insider status to bypass security measures and carry out their malicious activities without raising suspicion.

Impact: The consequences of insider attacks can be severe, ranging from financial losses and damage to the company's reputation to legal repercussions and regulatory fines.

As a board director, it's essential to recognize the threat posed by insider attacks and implement measures to prevent, detect, and respond to such incidents, including robust access controls, employee monitoring, and regular security awareness training.

Solution:

A solution to prevent insider threats involves a multi-layered approach that combines technology, policies, and organizational practices:

Access Control	Implement principle of least privilege to limit employees' access to sensitive data and systems based on their roles and responsibilities.
User Monitoring	Monitor user activities, including file access, system logins, and network traffic, to detect suspicious behaviour or deviations from normal patterns.
Employee Training	Provide comprehensive training and awareness programs to educate employees about the risks of insider threats and the importance of security policies and procedures.
Data Loss Prevention (DLP)	Deploy DLP solutions to monitor, detect, and prevent unauthorized transmission of sensitive data outside the organization's network.
Behavioural Analytics	Utilize behavioural analytics and machine learning algorithms to identify anomalous behaviour and potential insider threats based on patterns of activity.
Incident Response Plan	Develop and regularly test an incident response plan to quickly detect, investigate, and respond to insider threats when they occur.
Whitelisting and Blacklisting	Implement whitelisting and blacklisting measures to control the use of applications and devices within the organization's network.
Encryption	Encrypt sensitive data both at rest and in transit to protect it from unauthorized access, even in the event of insider threats.
Employee Screening	Conduct thorough background checks and screening processes before hiring employees to reduce the risk of insider threats.

Culture of Trust and Accountability	Foster a culture of trust, transparency, and accountability within the organization to encourage employees to report suspicious behaviour and adhere to security policies.

5. Password attacks

Scenario: Imagine a scenario where someone is trying to break into your company's network by testing a single, commonly used password across multiple user accounts. This is what we call a password spraying attack.

Modus Operandi: Instead of attempting to guess a specific user's password, like in a traditional brute force attack, a password spraying attack involves trying a small number of commonly used passwords against many accounts simultaneously.

This method reduces the risk of triggering account lockouts or detection by security systems. These common previously used passwords can be gathered from plethora of data breaches in past.

Impact: Think of it as trying a master key on multiple doors in hopes of finding one that unlocks. If successful, the attacker gains unauthorized access to sensitive company information or systems, potentially leading to data breaches, financial economic loss, or reputational damage.

Solution:

Take proactive measures to strengthen password policies, such as enforcing complex passwords and implementing multi-factor authentication, to mitigate the risk of unauthorized access to company resources.

6. Credential stuffing attacks

Scenario: For the sake of understanding, just imagine you use the same username and password for multiple online accounts, from your email to your social media profiles. Now, suppose a cybercriminal obtains a list of usernames and passwords from a data breach on one of such websites.

With this information, they attempt to log in to various other websites using the same credentials. This is what we call a credential stuffing attack.

Modus Operandi: For example, let's say your email and password were exposed in a data breach on a popular shopping website. A cybercriminal could then use automated tools to systematically try logging in to other websites, such as your online banking or social media accounts, using the same credentials.

Since many people reuse passwords across multiple accounts, this method often yields successful logins, giving attackers access to sensitive information or the ability to take over accounts.

Impact: You can check if your email has been involved in a data breach on websites like "haveibeenpwned.com," which aggregates data breach information and allows users to check if their email addresses have been compromised.

This tool can help you identify if your credentials have been exposed and take steps to secure your accounts, such as changing passwords and enabling multi-factor authentication.

Solution:

To protect against the risk of credential stuffing attacks and safeguard sensitive information from unauthorized access:

1. Essential to follow good password hygiene practices including usage of unique, complex passwords for each online account and avoiding password reuse across multiple platforms
2. Enable multi-factor authentication (MFA) whenever possible as an extra layer of security
3. Implement rate limiting and account lockout mechanisms to deter automated login attempts and monitor for suspicious login activity
4. Regularly monitor and update security measures

7. Social engineering attacks

Scenario: Social engineering or human hacking is a tactic used by cybercriminals to manipulate people into divulging confidential information or performing actions that compromise security. It relies on exploiting human psychology and trust to deceive individuals into providing access to sensitive data or systems.

Modus Operandi: These attackers may impersonate trusted entities, such as colleagues, vendors, or even authority figures, to trick their targets into disclosing passwords, financial information, or other sensitive data. They may also use techniques like pretexting, where they create a false scenario to gain the target's trust and cooperation.

Impact: Think of it as someone putting on a convincing disguise to gain access to a restricted area. In the digital realm, social engineers disguise their true intentions to gain access to valuable information or systems.

Solution:

Educate employees about common tactics used by attackers, such as phishing emails, phone scams, and impersonation techniques.

Implementing security awareness training and establishing clear procedures for verifying requests for sensitive information can help mitigate the risk of falling victim to social engineering attacks.

8. Business Email Compromise (BEC) attacks

Scenario: I'm sure you've heard attacks where a fake CEO has sent out email to staff asking staff members to urgently transfer funds to a vendor's account to finalize an important business deal.

The gullible staff member follows the instructions, only to later discover that the email was not actually from the CEO, but from a cybercriminal who had infiltrated into their email account. This is what we call a Business Email Compromise (BEC) attack.

Modus Operandi: In a BEC attack, also known as fake CEO fraud or email account compromise, cybercriminals impersonate a trusted individual within an organization, such as a CEO, CFO, or other executive, to deceive employees into taking unauthorized actions, such as transferring funds, sharing sensitive information, or initiating wire transfers.

Impact: These attackers often conduct thorough reconnaissance to gather information about their targets, such as email addresses, job titles, and organizational hierarchies, to craft convincing emails that appear legitimate. They may also spoof email addresses or use social engineering tactics to manipulate employees into complying with their fraudulent requests.

Think of it as someone wearing a convincing disguise to trick you into handing over sensitive information or performing financial transactions, unaware that you're being deceived.

Solution:

Implementing strong email technical security measures:

- Multi-factor authentication
- Email authentication protocols (SPF, DKIM, DMARC)
- Employee training to recognize phishing attempts
- Verify the authenticity of email requests

can help mitigate the risk of falling victim to BEC attacks.

Implementing strong email operational security measures:

- Establish clear procedures to verify and approve financial transactions, especially those initiated via email
- Enforce a maker-checker methodology to double check outbound financial transactions
- Conduct a review of financial transactions to identify fraud in the initial stages (if any)

can help prevent unauthorized transfers of funds.

9. Man-in-the-middle (MitM) attacks

These days it's also known as Adversary-in-the-middle (AitM) to keep it gender neutral.

Scenario: In a MitM/AitM attack, a cybercriminal positions themselves between two parties who are communicating with each other, such as between your device and the internet, or between two systems within a network.

Modus Operandi: From this vantage point, the attacker can eavesdrop on the communication, intercept sensitive information like login credentials or financial details, and even manipulate the data being exchanged without either party's knowledge.

Impact: Think of it like someone tapping into your phone call and silently listening in on your conversation, except in the digital world, where it's your data that's being intercepted and potentially compromised.

Solution:

Understanding MitM attacks is crucial for safeguarding your company's sensitive information and maintaining the trust of your customers and partners. Implementing encryption protocols, using secure communication channels, and regularly monitoring network traffic can help detect and prevent MitM attacks.

10.　　DoS / DDoS attacks

Scenario: Consider someone clogging the entrance to your store with so many customers that no one else can get in, disrupting your business operations and causing frustration for your customers.

Modus Operandi: In a DoS attack, a cybercriminal floods a target server, network, or website with an overwhelming amount of traffic or requests, causing it to become unavailable to legitimate users.

This flood of traffic can be generated from a lone source, like a botnet-controlled army of compromised computers, or multiple sources distributed across the internet in a DDoS attack.

Impact: A critical resource suddenly becomes inaccessible to customers, or online services slows down to a crawl until they eventually grind to a halt because millions of legitimate appearing communication are initiated with your resource.

This is termed a Denial of Service (DoS). When the attack originates from numerous locations then it's termed as Distributed Denial of Service (DDoS) attack.

Solution:

Implement robust network security measures, such as firewalls, intrusion detection systems, and partnering with DDoS mitigation services. They can help mitigate the DoS/DDoS impact and keep your digital assets secure.

11.   Zero-day exploits

Scenario: Picture a timeline where Day 0 marks the moment when the vulnerability is identified by software developers or security researchers. From this point onward, there are "zero days" available for organizations to prepare defences or apply patches before cyber attackers begin exploiting the flaw.

Zero-day vulnerabilities are named as such because they represent a critical gap in time between the discovery of a software flaw and the release of a vendor patch to fix it.

This immediacy underscores the urgency and challenge of addressing zero-day vulnerabilities, as organizations must rapidly respond to threats without the luxury of advance notice or preparation time.

Modus Operandi: It's like a burglar finding a hidden entryway into your home that even you didn't know about, allowing them to break in undetected and steal your valuables. This is what we call an attack using zero-day exploit.

Impact: Cybercriminals exploit zero-day vulnerabilities to launch attacks before the developers even know they exist, giving them the upper hand in breaching systems and causing damage.

Solution:

Implementing proactive security measures, such as regular software updates, intrusion detection systems, and threat intelligence sharing, can help mitigate the risk of falling victim to these stealthy attacks.

12.   Advanced Persistent Threats (APTs)

Scenario: An APT is a type of cyber-attack in which a well-funded and organized adversary, such as a nation-state or a highly skilled threat actors, deliberately targets a specific organization over an extended period.

Unlike opportunistic attacks, which may strike randomly, APTs are carefully planned and executed with the goal of remaining undetected for as long as possible.

Think of it as a skilled spy infiltrating your company, patiently gathering information, and planning their moves over time, all while remaining hidden from view.

Advanced:

Characterized by their advanced and sophisticated nature, often leveraging cutting-edge techniques and technologies to bypass traditional security measures. These attackers may employ custom-designed malware, zero-day exploits, and sophisticated social engineering tactics to achieve their objectives.

Persistent:

Unlike typical cyber-attacks, which may be opportunistic and short-lived, APTs are persistent in nature. The attackers are patient and persistent, often remaining undetected within the target network for months or even years, continuously gathering intelligence and carrying out their objectives over an extended period.

Threat:

APTs pose a significant and ongoing threat to organizations, as they are often well-funded, highly motivated, and have specific objectives in mind. These objectives may include espionage, intellectual property theft, financial gain, or sabotage, depending on the goals of the attackers.

Key Characteristics:

Targeted: APTs are typically targeted against specific organizations or industries, rather than indiscriminate attacks against random victims.

Stealthy: APTs are designed to operate stealthily, minimizing their footprint, and avoiding detection by traditional security controls.

Multi-Stage: APTs often involve multiple stages, including reconnaissance, initial infiltration, establishment of foothold, lateral movement within the network, and exfiltration of data.

Adaptability: APT attackers are adaptable and agile, capable of adjusting their tactics, techniques, and procedures (TTPs) in response to changes in the target's defences or environment.

Detection and Mitigation:

Detection of APTs can be challenging due to their stealthy and persistent nature. Organizations must invest in advanced threat detection technologies, such as endpoint detection and response (EDR) systems, network traffic analysis, and behaviour-based analytics, to identify suspicious activity indicative of an APT.

Mitigation of APTs requires a multi-layered approach to cybersecurity, including proactive defence measures such as threat intelligence sharing, security awareness training, regular security assessments, and incident response planning.

Solution:

To better prepare themselves to detect, mitigate, and respond to these sophisticated cyber threats effectively, understanding the characteristics and tactics of APTs is crucial.

Implementing robust cybersecurity measures, such as network segmentation, intrusion detection systems, and employee training on recognizing suspicious activity, can help detect and mitigate the risk of APTs.

Additionally, establishing incident response plans and regularly conducting security assessments can help organizations respond effectively in the event of an APT attack.

13.   Supply chain attacks

Scenario: Think of it as someone tampering with a product during the manufacturing process, inserting a hidden vulnerability that remains undetected until it's too late.

Modus Operandi: A supply chain attack occurs when cybercriminals target the software, hardware, or services provided by third-party vendors or suppliers to gain unauthorized access to the networks or systems of their customers.

Impact: These attackers exploit the trust established between the target organization and its suppliers, leveraging the supply chain as a vector to infiltrate and compromise the target's infrastructure.

Solution:

Following methods can help mitigate the impact of and respond effectively to in the event of a supply chain breach:

- Implementing supply chain risk management practices, such as vetting and monitoring third-party vendors
- Conducting security assessments
- Implementing contractual obligations for security standards
- Establishing incident response plans
- Maintaining open communication with suppliers can help organizations

14.   IoT device based attack

Scenario: World today is fascinated with internet enabled and "smart" labelled devices. like security cameras, speakers, vacuum cleaners, fridges, thermostats, and other Internet enabled devices.

These devices can be used as attack vector like suddenly start acting strangely, sending unusual data packets across your network, or even participating in a large-scale cyber-attack without your knowledge. This is what we call an IoT device-based attack.

Modus Operandi: In an IoT device-based attack, cybercriminals exploit vulnerabilities in connected devices including industrial sensors, to gain unauthorized access to your network or launch malicious activities.

Impact: These attacks can range from simple intrusions, like unauthorized access to sensitive data, to more sophisticated attacks, such as distributed denial of service (DDoS) attacks using compromised IoT devices as part of a botnet.

Solution:
Implementing strict security measures for IoT devices such as ones listed below can help mitigate the risk of unauthorized access and exploitation include:

- Changing default passwords
- Regularly updating firmware
- Segmenting IoT networks from critical systems
- Conducting thorough security assessments of IoT devices before deployment
- Monitoring network traffic for unusual behaviour can help detect and respond to potential threats in a timely manner

15. Web and Mobile app vulnerabilities

Scenario: Your company most probably would have developed (inhouse or outsourced) a cutting-edge web application or mobile application that serves as the backbone of your company's operations, handling sensitive data and facilitating critical transactions.

Modus Operandi: In a web and API attack, cybercriminals target weaknesses in the code, configuration, or implementation of web applications and APIs to compromise the security of your systems.

These attacks can take various forms, including injection attacks (such as SQL injection or cross-site scripting), authentication bypass, insecure direct object references, and data exfiltration.

Impact: Cybercriminals exploiting vulnerabilities in your application's web and API interfaces to gain unauthorized access, steal confidential information, or disrupt services.

Solution:

Implementing secure coding practices, conducting regular security assessments and penetration testing commonly knows these days as VAPT, and staying informed about emerging threats and vulnerabilities in web technologies can help mitigate the risk of exploitation.

These tests should be done in line with OWASP top10 issues in Web, Mobile and APIs

Additionally, leveraging security technologies such as web application firewalls (WAFs) and API gateways can provide an additional layer of defence against malicious actors attempting to exploit vulnerabilities in your systems.

16.   Nation State Attack

Scenario: Nation state attacks are incredibly sophisticated since they are planned over a long time and executed with precision to avoid detection.

This is not your average cyber-attack; think:

- Large scale critical infrastructure outages
- Military/government espionage and data theft
- Riots encouraged over social media
- Deepfake AI generated videos
- Spreading misinformation
- Data exfiltration
- Modifying formulas for healthcare drugs
- Unsanctioned spying of persons of interest (journalists, politicians, military personnel etc) via their laptops/mobile.
- Stock market scams, global banking theft
- and the list just goes on

For obvious reasons, no government or government sponsored entity will ever admit that they carried out a cyber-attack.

Modus Operandi: To conduct attacks of such magnitude detailed recces are carried out, software vulnerabilities exploited, malware / virus developed, physical access points identified just to name a few.

The overall attack is designed to slip in and out without detection and leave no trace of its existence like a top-secret military operation in another country.

Certain countries allocate significant resources towards clandestine government entities and/or private organizations who then develop, deploy, and maintain such an attack infrastructure.

Sometimes it's so brazen that such attack infrastructure is even commercially sold; and we have all heard about the Pegasus tool used for espionage purposes.

Impact: The consequences are truly devastating:

- Large scale deaths or targeted assassinations
- Crippling of critical support infrastructure
- Toppling governments by fake news campaigns on social media
- Blackmail, extortion over public data leaks
- Manipulating operations for military defence contractors
- and the list just goes on.

Solution:

Mitigating such attacks is difficult but not impossible. It needs diligent deployment, fine-tuning of tools and platforms followed by strict monitoring for any security incidents.

If you have reason to believe that you could be a target for a nation state attack, then it is critical that you employ all the strategy and tactics outlined in this book with 100% dedication and efficiency.

It would be prudent to presume that if you are a government entity or an independent organization working on cutting-edge technology, government contracts, military data etc, then your threat perception will be at elevated levels.

Given the above work environment it would be very unwise to turn complacent over time. You must have a dedicated information security team working 24x7 tasked with protecting your infrastructure.

Resources obtained are directed at research, hiring personnel, equipment etc, but very often we see that deployment of cyber security controls takes a back seat allowing easy ingress into the data vaults of entities.

Perform a threat assessment study and Business impact analysis to understand your risk areas. Treat your IT infrastructure, processes, and relevant data with extra precaution for high-risk areas.

Chapter 17

Understanding Security Keywords

As we said earlier, cyber security comprises of an ocean of keywords and would require a separate chapter. Let's look at some of the technologies and how they provide value. This may help you prioritise them based on your risk appetite.

Here's a list of technical solutions commonly used in cybersecurity.

1. Security Architectures

Threat Modelling

Threat modelling is a structured approach to assessing the security risks associated with a system or application by analysing potential threats, their potential impact, and the likelihood of occurrence.

When developing a new software application, threat modelling involves identifying potential attack vectors, such as unauthorized access, data breaches, or denial-of-service attacks. By understanding these threats, developers can implement security controls and design features that mitigate risks and protect against potential vulnerabilities.

Zero Trust Architecture (ZTA)

Zero Trust architecture is about not automatically trusting anyone or anything inside or outside the network, and instead verifying everything that tries to connect to our systems. It's a security approach that ensures continuous verification and strict access controls, regardless of the user's location or device.

Hence, even if an employee is working from their usual office network, they would still need to authenticate themselves before accessing sensitive company data or applications, just as they would if they were working remotely from a coffee shop.

2. Security Concepts

Malware

Short for MALicious softWARE, it's commonly used for virus, trojan, spyware, etc. It is any software designed to intentionally cause financial damage, data theft, endpoint corruption, privacy breaches, or gain unauthorized access to computer systems.

Malware can be distributed through various vectors such as email attachments, malicious websites, infected USB drives, and software vulnerabilities.

Ransomware

Ransomware is type of malware that encrypts files or locks access to a system. Attackers demand payment (ransom) to restore access or decrypt files. It's often spread through phishing emails, malicious attachments, or exploit kits.

Threat Actor

First thing first, hackers are the good guys, an attacker is a threat actor.

A threat actor could be an individual, group, or entity that initiates or carries out malicious activities against an organization or its assets. Threat actors can include cybercriminals, hacktivists, nation-state actors, and insiders.

Their motivations vary and may include financial gain, espionage, sabotage, ideological reasons, or personal vendettas. Understanding the capabilities, tactics, techniques, and procedures (TTPs) of threat actors is crucial for effective cybersecurity defence.

Threat intelligence gathering helps identify and mitigate potential threats posed by various threat actors.

Social Engineering

Social engineering is a manipulation technique used to deceive individuals into divulging confidential information, performing actions, or giving access to systems. It exploits human psychology rather than technical vulnerabilities.

Common tactics include phishing emails, pretexting, baiting, and tailgating. Attackers aim to gain trust or exploit emotions to achieve their goals, such as obtaining passwords, financial information, or unauthorized access. Social engineering attacks can occur via various communication channels, including phone calls, emails, and in-person interactions.

Brute Force Attack

A brute force attack is a trial-and-error method used to obtain information, such as a password or encryption key. It involves systematically checking all combinations until the correct one is found.

Brute force attacks can be time-consuming and resource-intensive, but highly effective against weak or easily guessable passwords. Attackers combine automated tools, powerful hardware, and intelligent software to rapidly generate and test millions of combinations.

Darkweb / Darknet

The darkweb/darknet is a hidden marketplace, accessible only through specialized software, where users mostly engage in illicit activities, trade illegal goods and services anonymously. Darknet is not indexed by traditional search engines and requires specific tools like Tor to access.

Users can access darkweb marketplaces to purchase drugs, stolen credit card information, or hacking tools, often using cryptocurrencies like Bitcoin to facilitate transactions. The anonymity provided by the dark web makes it attractive to criminals looking to evade detection and law enforcement authorities.

While the darkweb can be a breeding ground for criminal activities, it's essential to understand that not everything on the dark web is illegal. Some users utilize it for privacy-preserving purposes, such as anonymous communication or accessing censored information.

Network Segmentation

Involves dividing a network into smaller segments or zones to control and restrict the flow of traffic and limit the impact of security incidents. Think of server segment, user segment, admin segment.

Commonly known as VLAN

MicroSegmentation

Micro Segmentation is partitioning your organization's network into smaller, more manageable segments to control and monitor traffic flow. At times we can segregate to a point of isolating individual endpoints.

Modify granularity like which server can talk to which other server on which specific port only. This way lateral attacks can be prevented as you are allowing only required traffic and blocking rest. Consider this as VLAN going even granular.

Deep Packet Inspection (DPI)

Deep Packet Inspection (DPI) is an advanced network monitoring and security technique that examines data passing through a network at the packet level, and provides insights into the types of traffic, applications, and protocols being used.

DPI works by inspecting data packets contents to identify specific applications, websites, or even malware signatures.

For example, if a user is streaming a video, DPI can detect the streaming protocol used, the video resolution, and the amount of data transferred. If the network administrator wants to block access to certain websites or prioritize critical applications, DPI can help enforce policies based on this information.

Cyber Threat Intelligence

Cyber Threat Intelligence (CTI) is like having a crystal ball for cybersecurity. It allows information gathering about potential cyber threats and insight into how they might affect our organization. This educates us about the latest tricks and schemes cybercriminals use to try and infiltrate endpoints and steal data.

With CTI, we can identify patterns, trends, and emerging risks in our environment, allowing us to take proactive steps to protect our company's sensitive information and assets. Consider this a trusted advisor whispering in our ear, helping us stay one step ahead of the bad guys.

Deception Technology

Deception technology is like setting up honeypots, digital traps, and decoys within your organization's network to lure and deceive cyber attackers, diverting their attention away from valuable assets and providing early warning of potential breaches.

For example, suppose a cyber attacker infiltrates your network and begins searching for sensitive data. They encounter a decoy file labelled "Confidential Financial Documents" and attempt to access it. Instantly, an alert is triggered, notifying security personnel of the unauthorized activity, and providing valuable insights into the attacker's tactics and objectives.

Deception technology also helps organizations gather threat intelligence by analysing attacker behaviour and techniques. By understanding how adversaries operate, organizations can strengthen their defences, patch vulnerabilities, and proactively prevent future attacks.

Data Masking

Data masking is a data security technique that replaces real data with fictional or obscured data, making it unreadable or unintelligible to unauthorized users while preserving its usability for legitimate purposes. Data masking works by hiding or altering certain data elements so only authorized individuals can access the original information.

If a database contains customer credit card numbers, data masking could replace the actual card numbers with fake numbers that look similar but are not valid. This way, developers or testers working with the database can still perform their tasks without exposing sensitive information.

Data Anonymization

Data anonymization is stripping away personal identifiers from datasets to protect individuals' privacy while still allowing for analysis and research. It's a technique used to remove or obfuscate information that could be used to identify individuals, such as names, addresses, or social security numbers, from a dataset.

For example, in a healthcare dataset, personal identifiers like patients' names and social security numbers may be replaced with unique identifiers, and dates of birth may be generalized to age ranges. This allows researchers to analyse health trends and outcomes without compromising patients' privacy.

Data Integrity

Data integrity is ensuring the reliability, accuracy, and consistency of data throughout its lifecycle. In a database, data integrity mechanisms such as validation rules, checksums, and cryptographic hashing can be used to verify the accuracy and consistency of data. This helps detect and prevent errors or tampering that could compromise data reliability.

Data Sovereignty

Data sovereignty is the concept of digital independence, where a country or organization asserts control and jurisdiction over the data generated within its borders or by its citizens. It refers to the legal and regulatory framework governing the collection, storage, processing, and transfer of data, ensuring that data remains subject to the laws and regulations of the jurisdiction where it originates.

Data sovereignty regulations may require organizations to store sensitive data within the country's borders, restrict the transfer of certain types of data across international borders, or impose data localization requirements to ensure that data remains under national jurisdiction.

Data Classification

Data classification is the process of categorizing data based on its sensitivity, value, or regulatory requirements. It helps organizations prioritize protection measures and determine appropriate access controls.

Common classifications include public, internal use only, confidential, and sensitive. Data classification policies typically outline criteria for classification and specify handling procedures for each category.

Classification can be based on factors like regulatory compliance, business impact, and confidentiality requirements.

One can also opt for Traffic Light Protocol by first.org for data classification.

Multi-factor Authentication (MFA)

Authentication methods that require users to provide multiple forms of verification, such as passwords, biometrics, or security tokens, to access systems or applications.

Single factor: What you know – a username and password

2nd factor: What you have – a token or phone number or a smart device, even biometric (which many times is called as MFA)

Multifactor: When more than 2 factors are used – like OTP + fingerprint

Today 2FA & MFA are often used interchangeably.

Passwordless Authentication

This is an authentication method allowing users to access their accounts without relying on passwords, using alternative factors such as:

Biometric Authentication: users can unlock their devices or log into applications using fingerprints, facial recognition, or iris scans.

Security Keys: users can authenticate themselves by plugging in a physical USB key or using a Bluetooth-enabled device.

Device-based Authentication: relies on the possession and security of the user's trusted device, such as a smartphone or smartwatch.

Single Sign On (SSO)

A methodology where every system of the enterprise uses same central username and password database. Consider one employee one password which can help them login to ERP, HRMS, mails, file server, and many more services. When the credentials are changed or access is revoked, the changes are reflected across all relevant applications.

Adaptive Authentication

Adaptive Authentication dynamically assesses the risk associated with each authentication attempt and applies appropriate security measures accordingly. For a user authenticating from a familiar device, location, and during regular business hours, Adaptive Authentication may require only a username and password for verification.

However, if the same user tries to log in from an unfamiliar device, location, or at an unusual time, Adaptive Authentication may prompt for additional factors, such as a one-time passcode sent to their registered email or phone.

This prevents unauthorized access to systems if credentials ever get compromised.

Domain-Based Message Authentication, Reporting, and Conformance (DMARC)

Domain-based Message Authentication, Reporting, and Conformance (DMARC) is an email authentication protocol allowing domain owners to specify how their email should be handled by recipient servers.

A company might implement a DMARC policy instructing recipient servers to reject or quarantine emails that fail authentication checks, helping to prevent malicious actors from impersonating their domain and sending fraudulent emails.

DomainKeys Identified Mail (DKIM)

DomainKeys Identified Mail (DKIM) is adding a digital signature to your emails, providing a way for email recipients to verify messages originating from legitimate senders and haven't been tampered while in transit.

It's an email authentication method allowing a sender to digitally sign outgoing messages using cryptographic keys associated with their domain.

Sender Policy Framework (SPF)

Sender Policy Framework (SPF) is an email authentication protocol enabling domain owners to define which servers are allowed to send emails on behalf of their domain. SPF allows domain owners to create DNS record lists for authorized email servers, thereby preventing spammers from spoofing their domain.

Encryption Technologies

Techniques for securing data by encoding it such that only authorized parties can access and decipher the information. Mostly used for "data-at-rest" using full disk encryption (FDE) or for "data-in-motion" using SSL/TLS commonly seen in HTTPS

Quantum-Safe Cryptography

Quantum-Safe Cryptography is a branch of cryptography that focuses on developing algorithms and protocols resistant to attacks from quantum computers.

Its aiming to create cryptographic systems remaining secure even in the face of powerful quantum computers, which could someday render existing encryption methods obsolete.

3. Security Processes

Secure Data Erasure

This is a process of permanently removing data from storage devices rendering it irrecoverable, thus preventing unauthorized access to sensitive information.

When a storage device such as a hard drive or SSD is decommissioned, secure data erasure can be used to ensure that all data stored on the device is completely wiped out.

Process involves systematically overwriting the entire storage space with random data multiple times, making it virtually impossible for anyone to recover the original data.

Software Bill of Materials (SBOM)

Consider creating a detailed recipe for a complex dish, listing out all the ingredients, quantities, types, and their sources. Applying this to a software development environment creates a structured list providing comprehensive information about the software components used in an application or system, including their origins, versions, dependencies, and known vulnerabilities.

An ideal SBOM should include details such as the names and versions of libraries, frameworks, and modules used along with licensing patterns and known vulnerabilities.

This information enables organizations to assess the security posture of their software supply chain and make informed decisions about risk management and remediation strategies.

Secure Code Review

This process involves a cybersecurity expert meticulously inspecting your application source code to identify potential security vulnerabilities. Checks include improper input validation, insecure authentication mechanisms, or susceptibility to injection attacks. Adherence to industry standard secure coding practices and standards (OWASP, CERT) is also reviewed.

Appropriate mitigation strategies are identified and deployed to secure the code base.

Secure Software Development Lifecycle (SSDLC)

SSDLC focuses on building secure and resilient software applications. It integrates across the board from requirements gathering to deployment and maintenance.

Throughout the development process, security controls are implemented, code is rigorously tested for vulnerabilities, and security reviews are conducted to identify and mitigate potential risks.

Container Security

Containers are lightweight, portable, and efficient units of software packaging that bundle an application and its dependencies together. Container security focuses on protecting these containers and the applications they contain from various threats, vulnerabilities, and attacks.

Container security involves measures such as:

1. **Image Scanning:** Checking container images for vulnerabilities and misconfigurations before deployment.

2. Runtime Protection: Monitoring container activity during execution to detect and prevent malicious behaviour.

3. Access Control: Implementing strict access controls and permissions to limit who can interact with containers.

4. Network Segmentation: Isolating containers from each other and from external networks to minimize the risk of lateral movement by attackers.

5. Compliance Monitoring: Ensuring that containers adhere to security policies, regulatory requirements, and best practices.

Breach and Attack Simulation (BAS)

Similar to a cybersecurity fire drill for your organization, BAS involves testing your defence, response, and resilience capabilities by simulating real-world cyber-attacks.

During a BAS exercise, security professionals mimic the tactics and techniques of cyber attackers, attempt network infiltration leading to sensitive data compromise. Tactics could involve sending phishing emails, malware injections, or exploiting vulnerabilities in your systems.

By simulating various real-world attack scenarios, organizations can:

- Evaluate their detection and response procedures
- Train their security teams
- Implement necessary improvements

4. Security Monitoring

Security Information and Event Management (SIEM) Systems

Software solutions that collect, analyse, and correlate security event data from various sources to identify and respond to security incidents. Can be thought as central log management system.

Logs source could include Anti-malware, Active Directory, Firewall, WiFi Access Points, Web applications, Cloud environments, Email etc.

Security Orchestration, Automation, and Response (SOAR) Platforms

It is a technological framework designed to enhance the efficiency and effectiveness of security operations by integrating multiple security tools and processes. It combines 3 segments:

- Orchestration: involves coordinating various security technologies
- Automation: reduces need for manual intervention by automating repetitive tasks
- Response: streamlines and accelerates the response to security incidents.

SOAR platforms enable security teams to detect, manage, and respond to threats more quickly and accurately, improving overall incident response times and reducing the impact of security breaches.

They also help in standardizing and enforcing security processes, thereby enhancing compliance and governance.

Security Operations Center (SOC)

A service where a team monitors all the security activity, using a SIEM platform, raises alerts, and mitigates the threat. Could be a 24x7 operation. Large companies tend to create this inhouse, most MSME, SME, SMB prefer to outsource.

Threat Intelligence Feeds

A Threat Intelligence Feed is a continuous stream of updates on potential cyber threats delivered straight to your dashboard. It's akin to a digital news ticker, but instead of headlines, it delivers alerts about new malware strains, hacking methods, or vulnerabilities that could pose risks to your organization.

For example, if a new phishing campaign is detected targeting organizations in your industry, the Threat Intelligence Feed will alert you to the specific email addresses, domains, or IP addresses associated with the attack.

Armed with this information, you can proactively block malicious traffic, update security policies, or educate employees to recognize and avoid phishing attempts.

Threat Attribution

It is possible to trace (with some confidence) cyber threats back to their source, whether they are individual threat actor, organized crime groups, nation-states, or other malicious actors.

It involves a detailed analysis of the code and infrastructure used in an attack, examining tactics and techniques associated with known threat actors, and correlating attack patterns with previous incidents or threat intelligence reports.

A key factor involves collaborating with law enforcement agencies, cybersecurity researchers, and industry partners to share information and receive insights.

Attack Surface Monitoring

A proactive approach to cybersecurity involving continuous monitoring and assessment of an organizations exposed attack surface. It allows an organization to take steps to mitigate potential identified security risks.

Attack surface monitoring may involve scanning internet-facing assets such as websites, servers, and databases for vulnerabilities and misconfigurations. It may also include monitoring social media channels, public repositories, and other sources for leaked credentials or sensitive information that could be exploited by attackers.

Threat Hunting

Threat hunting is like playing detective in your organization's network, actively searching for signs of hidden threats and potential security breaches. Threat hunters use advanced techniques and tools to proactively seek out threats by analysing network traffic, log data, and endpoint activity for any signs of malicious activity.

By uncovering these threats before they escalate into full-blown attacks, threat hunting helps organizations stay one step ahead of cyber adversaries.

Threat Intelligence Platforms (TIP)

A platform to collect, manage and act upon the threat intelligence gathered from various free and paid sources. By aggregating and contextualizing threat intelligence, TIPs empower organizations to make informed decisions and proactively defend against cyber-attacks.

They provide valuable insights into adversaries' tactics, techniques, and procedures, enabling organizations to anticipate and counter emerging threats effectively.

Threat Intelligence Sharing

Threat Intelligence Sharing is like having a neighbourhood watch program for the digital world, where organizations collaborate to share information (insights, indicators, analysis and more) about cyber threats and attacks for the collective good.

For example, if one organization detects a new type of malware or identifies a phishing campaign targeting their industry, they can share this information with other organizations through threat intelligence sharing platforms or networks. This allows other organizations to take proactive measures to defend against the same threat, such as updating their security controls or blocking malicious IP addresses.

Managed Security Service Provider (MSSP)

This is like having a dedicated team of cybersecurity experts on standby, ready to protect your organization's digital assets and infrastructure around the clock.

MSSPs offer a wide range of services, including threat detection and response, security monitoring, vulnerability management, and compliance assistance.

By partnering with an MSSP, organizations can:

- Access advanced security capabilities and stay ahead of evolving cyber threats without the need for extensive in-house resources.
- MSSPs leverages specialized tools, expertise, and industry best practices to proactively identify and mitigate security threats, minimizing the risk of data breaches and disruptions to business operations. MSSPs offer scalable solutions tailored to the specific needs and risk profile of each organization, providing peace of mind, and enabling focus on core business objectives.

Network Security Policy Management

It is critical to understand the creation, enforcement, and maintenance of policies that dictate how network resources should be accessed, used, and protected. Network Security Policy Management works by establishing rules and configurations for controlling access, preventing unauthorized activities, and responding to security incidents within your network.

Network security policies may specify which users or devices are allowed to connect to the network, what types of traffic are permitted or blocked, and how sensitive data should be encrypted and transmitted.

These policies are enforced by security devices such as firewalls, intrusion detection systems, and access control mechanisms.

5. Security Assessment

Red Teaming

Red teaming refers to the offensive side of cybersecurity operations. This akin to staging a realistic cyber-attack on your own organization to identify vulnerabilities and weaknesses in your security defences. It's a proactive and strategic approach to cybersecurity by simulating the tactics, techniques, and procedures (TTPs) of real-world adversaries to assess your security control effectiveness.

Activities include:

- Conducting phishing campaigns to trick employees into divulging sensitive information
- Attempting to exploit vulnerabilities in your network infrastructure
- Physically breach your premises to assess the effectiveness of physical security measures

The goal is to identify weaknesses before malicious attackers can exploit them and provide actionable recommendations for improvement.

Blue Teaming

Blue teaming refers to the defensive side of cybersecurity operations. They are responsible for protecting an organization's systems, networks, and data from cyber threats.

Activities include such as vulnerability assessments, threat hunting, and incident response.

Blue teams (researchers) often work closely with red teams (attackers) in simulated exercises called "red team-blue team" exercises to test and improve defences.

The goal is to detect, prevent, and mitigate cyber threats effectively to ensure the security and resilience of the organization's assets.

Purple Teaming

Purple teaming (Red + Blue makes Purple) combines elements of both red teaming (offensive) and blue teaming (defensive) in cybersecurity. It involves collaborative exercises where red and blue teams work together to improve overall security posture.

Red teams simulate attacks, while blue teams defend against them. Unlike traditional red team-blue team exercises, purple teaming emphasizes communication and knowledge sharing between the two teams.

It helps identify weaknesses in defences, validate security controls, and enhance incident response capabilities effectively.

Vulnerability Management

A platform to scan for vulnerabilities in your systems, applications, and network infrastructure, to tell you what's wrong, where, and track remediation for the same. Priorities for each identified vulnerability allow remediation of severe impact issues before others.

6. Security Protocols

Virtual Private Networks (VPNs)

Encrypted connections over public networks, allowing remote users to access private networks securely. Basically, creating a secure tunnel of communication in an insecure environment like public internet.

Secure Socket Layer (SSL) & Transport Layer Security (TLS)

Cryptographic solutions providing encryption, authentication, and integrity for data transmitted between your device and a web server. SSL and TLS operate similarly, wrapping (encrypting) your data in layers of protection before sending it over the internet.

SSL was the original protocol designed to secure online communication, but it has been replaced by its successor, TLS. TLS builds upon the foundation of SSL and offers stronger security features and improved performance.

For example, when you visit a secure website (indicated by "https://" in the URL), your web browser and the server negotiate a secure connection using TLS. This process involves exchanging digital certificates to verify the server identity to establish a secure channel for encrypted data transmission.

Secure Shell (SSH)

Cryptographic network protocol providing a secure channel for remotely accessing and managing devices over an unsecured network, such as the internet.

If you need to remotely access your company's server to troubleshoot an issue or deploy updates, you can use SSH to establish a secure connection. This connection encrypts all data transmitted between your computer and the server, protecting it from interception or tampering by cybercriminals.

Secure File Transfer Protocol (SFTP)

Protocol used for transferring files securely between a client and a server, providing encryption and authentication mechanisms to safeguard data integrity and confidentiality using SSH as an underlying protocol.

When you upload a file using SFTP, data is encrypted before being sent over the network, making it unreadable to anyone who intercepts it. SFTP requires users to authenticate themselves using credentials such as usernames and passwords or cryptographic keys, ensuring only authorized individuals can access the files.

7. Security Platforms

Firewalls (FW)

Network security devices that monitor and control incoming and outgoing network traffic based on predetermined security rules. Firewall is a hardware device placed at your network perimeter where the internet provider line drops, and corporate connection starts.

Software firewalls are gaining traction in certain environments. Endpoints have software firewalls deployed for local protection. Like Windows Firewall or Mac OS firewall.

Hardware firewalls are called Network firewalls, and software firewalls are called Host firewalls.

Next-Generation Firewall (NGFW)

Next-Generation Firewall (NGFW) represents the evolution of traditional firewall technology, offering advanced capabilities beyond traditional protections like basic firewalls that filter traffic based on IP addresses and ports.

NGFW takes this defence to the next level by incorporating advanced features such as application awareness, intrusion prevention, and integrated threat intelligence.

For example, while traditional firewalls only inspect network traffic based on basic criteria, NGFW can identify and control specific applications, even if they use non-standard ports or protocols. It can also detect and block sophisticated attacks such as malware, command and control communication, and data exfiltration attempts.

Intrusion Prevention Systems (IPS)

Security appliances or software that monitor network traffic and "prevents" potential threats or attacks in real-time. With passage of times, IDS/IPS are not bundled by many vendors in one. Again, can be a hardware appliance or a software.

Intrusion Detection Systems (IDS)

Intrusion Detection Systems (IDS) are cybersecurity appliances designed to detect and alert you to potential security breaches or malicious activities within your network.

An IDS may flag anomalies such as repeated login attempts from unfamiliar IP addresses, unusual traffic patterns indicative of a denial-of-service attack, or unauthorized access attempts to sensitive files or directories. Upon detecting such activities, the IDS generates alerts or triggers automated responses to mitigate the threat and notify security personnel.

Software-Defined Perimeter (SDP)

Software-Defined Perimeter (SDP) provides a software-based approach to network access, dynamically restricting access to resources based on user identity and device security posture. This minimizes the attack surface and reduces the risk of unauthorized access.

Traditionally, networks were guarded by firewalls and VPNs. SDP takes this a step further by creating individualized perimeters for each user and device, regardless of their location.

When a user attempts to access a network resource, SDP evaluates their identity, device security status, and contextual factors like time of day or location.

Based on this assessment, SDP dynamically constructs a "perimeter" around the user, granting access only to the specific resources they need, while blocking access to all others.

Antivirus/Anti-malware Software

Software designed to detect, prevent, and remove malicious software such as viruses, worms, and Trojans from systems and networks.

It's a program designed to detect, prevent, and remove malicious software, or malware, from computers and other devices. It scans files and systems for known threats using signature-based detection and heuristic analysis to identify and neutralize viruses, worms, trojans, and other harmful programs. By regularly updating its virus definitions, antivirus software helps protect against emerging threats and provides a crucial layer of security to prevent data breaches, system corruption, and unauthorized access.

Endpoint Protection Platforms (EPP)

Security solutions that protect endpoints such as desktops, laptops, and mobile devices from malware, unauthorized access, and other security threats. It can be called as a level up for antivirus/antimalware.

Endpoint Protection Platforms (EPP) are comprehensive security solutions designed to protect endpoint devices, such as laptops, desktops, and mobile devices, from a wide range of threats. EPP combines traditional antivirus capabilities with additional security features like firewalls, intrusion detection and prevention, and behavioural analysis.

It provides a holistic approach to endpoint security, addressing both known and unknown threats by using advanced techniques like machine learning and threat intelligence to detect, block, and remediate malware, ransomware, and other cyber threats, ensuring robust protection for all endpoint devices in an organization.

Endpoint Detection and Response (EDR)

EDR is a cybersecurity technology that monitors devices for cyber threats like malware and ransomware. EDR solutions record and store endpoint behaviours, analyse data to identify suspicious activity, and block malicious activity. They also provide remediation suggestions to restore affected systems.

EDR differs from antivirus (AV) and anti-malware by not solely depending on heuristic or signature-based detection mechanisms.

Instead, it has capabilities like continuous monitoring, advanced threat detection, investigation & response capabilities for sophisticated attacks like ransomware.

Network Detection and Response (NDR)

Think of EDR above but for network traffic. Again, not the firewall we discussed before, but much more intelligent than that which can be an add-on to your next generation firewall (NGFW).

Network Detection and Response (NDR) is a solution focused on identifying and mitigating threats within an organization's network. Unlike traditional security measures that rely solely on predefined rules or signatures, NDR employs advanced analytics, machine learning, and behaviour analysis to detect anomalies and suspicious activities.

It continuously monitors network traffic in real-time, allowing for swift detection and response to potential intrusions with the power of threat intelligence. This enhances comprehensive network security by providing visibility into threats that might bypass other security layers.

Extended Detection and Response (XDR)

Imagine you have various security tools in place, such as endpoint protection, network security, and cloud security solutions, each generating its own alerts and data. XDR can be considered as EDR+NDR+SIEM+SOAR.

With XDR, all these security tools are connected and integrated into a single platform, providing a holistic view of your security posture. XDR collects and correlates data from various sources, identifying patterns and anomalies that may indicate a security threat. If a suspicious activity is detected, XDR automatically initiates a response, such as isolating a compromised device or blocking malicious traffic.

Secure Web Gateway (SWG)

SWG enforces security policies set by your organization, such as restricting access to certain websites or online services based on user roles, usage patterns, or time of day irrespective whether user is located on-premises or anywhere else.

Any deviation from these policies will result in alerts and visibility into reasons for the deviation. Administrators can take relevant mitigation action. Alternatively, the platform can perform proactive remediation measures automatically.

Cloud Access Security Broker (CASB)

CASB is like a gatekeeper for cloud applications, permitting only authorized users have access to company data stored in the cloud and monitoring for any suspicious activity.

CASBs can help protect corporate software-as-a-service (SaaS), infrastructure-as-a-service (IaaS), and platform-as-a-service (PaaS) applications from cyber-attacks and data leaks. They can also govern cloud usage based on identity, service, activity, application, and data.

Some features of a CASB include:

- Cloud governance and risk assessment

- Data loss prevention

- Control over native features of cloud services

- Threat prevention

- Configuration auditing

- Malware detection

- Data encryption and key management

Secure Access Service Edge (SASE)

SASE is like a security umbrella that protects users and data wherever they are, whether they're in the office, working from home, or accessing cloud applications on the go.

With SASE, all your traffic, including accessing cloud applications and internal resources, is routed through a centralized security platform. This platform applies consistent security policies, such as data encryption, threat detection, and access controls, regardless of your location or the device you're using.

So, even if you're working from an unsecured Wi-Fi network at coffee shops, airports, WiFi hotspot etc, SASE ensures that your data remains protected, and resources can be securely accessed to get your work done.

It simplifies security for both users and IT teams by providing comprehensive protection and visibility across the entire network and cloud infrastructure.

And no, it's not a VPN, its much beyond a VPN.

Password Manager

A password manager is a digital vault that securely stores and manages all your passwords in one place. It's a convenient and secure solution for individuals and organizations to generate, store, and autofill complex passwords across multiple accounts and devices.

It can automatically fill in your credentials on login pages, saving you time and effort while maintaining account security.

Some password managers also offer additional features such as password auditing, secure password sharing, and two-factor authentication integration.

Data Loss Prevention (DLP)

DLP is like a digital guardian that monitoring and controlling data flow across your network, cloud services, and endpoints, actively preventing unauthorized sharing, leakage, or theft of confidential data.

For instance, imagine your company deals with customer data, financial information, or intellectual property. DLP would scan emails, documents, and other digital assets to identify sensitive data, such as credit card numbers, personal identification information, or proprietary documents.

If an employee tries to send this sensitive data outside the company's network or upload it to a personal cloud storage service, DLP would intervene, either blocking the action altogether or prompting the employee to take necessary security measures, like encryption, before proceeding.

File Integrity Monitoring (FIM)

FIM detects any unauthorized changes in any critical file in real-time and alerts your security team, enabling them to investigate and respond swiftly to the potential breach.

FIM is essential for compliance with regulations like PCI DSS and HIPAA, which require organizations to maintain the integrity of sensitive data. By continuously monitoring file integrity, FIM helps organizations prevent data breaches, maintain regulatory compliance, and safeguard their digital assets.

Web Application Firewall (WAF)

Security appliances or software that monitor and filter HTTP/HTTPS traffic to protect web applications from common attacks such as SQL injection and cross-site scripting (XSS). Think of this as a firewall but only for web applications.

Lately, WAF is increasingly being deployed as a cloud service for ease of use and other factors. On-premises WAF devices are also available.

Network Access Control (NAC)

Security solutions that enforce policies for controlling access to network resources based on the identity, security posture, and compliance status of endpoints. A NAC denies non-corporate devices from accessing the corporate network. Isolates endpoints where policies such as (outdated patch/ antivirus update) are not met thereby reducing non-compliant devices from existing on the network leading to an enhanced security posture.

Privileged Access Management (PAM)

PAM is like having a secure vault for privileged users to store their credential/authentication keys to your organization's most sensitive assets, such as critical systems, servers, and confidential data.

For example, let's say an IT administrator needs to perform maintenance on a critical server. With PAM in place, administrator would request access to the server through the PAM system, which authenticates their identity and grants temporary access to the necessary resources. During the session, PAM continuously monitors the administrator's activities, recording all commands and changes made to the system for audit purposes.

PAM also enforces security policies, such as requiring multi-factor authentication and limiting access privileges based on job roles.

Secure Email Gateway (SEG)

SEG meticulously inspects incoming and outgoing emails to block malicious content and protects against email-based threats.

Email with a suspicious attachment or a link to a potentially harmful website will be intercepted by SEG before it reaches the recipient's inbox. Content will be analysed using various security measures such as antivirus scans, content filtering, and threat intelligence feeds.

If the email is deemed safe, it will be delivered to the recipient as usual. However, if it's identified as a threat, the SEG will quarantine or block the email and notify the administrator to take preventive action thereby protecting the organization.

Remote Browser Isolation (RBI)

With RBI, instead of accessing websites directly from your device, your web browsing session is conducted on a remote server or virtual machine in the cloud. When you click on a link or visit a website, RBI opens a virtual browser session in the cloud and streams the visual output back to your device.

Any threats such as drive-by downloads, zero-day exploits, and malicious code or malware encountered during your browsing session are neutralized or confined to the remote environment, preventing it from reaching your endpoint device.

Hardware Security Module (HSM)

HSM is a high-security vault for storing and managing cryptographic keys and sensitive data. It's a dedicated hardware device designed to perform cryptographic operations securely and protect critical assets from unauthorized access or tampering.

In a banking environment, an HSM might be used to generate and store encryption keys for securing online transactions, ensuring that customer data remains confidential and protected from cyber threats. Additionally, HSMs can enforce strict access controls and audit trails to monitor and track key usage.

Mobile Device Management (MDM)

MDM is a comprehensive solution to centrally manage and secure mobile endpoints, allowing you to enforce security policies, manage configurations, and protect sensitive data on smartphones, tablets, and other mobile devices.

With MDM, administrators can enforce password policies, encrypt device data, and restrict access to certain apps or websites, helping to prevent unauthorized access and mitigate the risk of data breaches. They can also deploy software updates and patches to ensure that devices are running the latest security fixes.

Unified Endpoint Management (UEM)

UEM is next level of MDM where UEM extends beyond mobile devices to encompass a wider range of endpoints, including laptops, desktops, and IoT devices.

UEM offers a broader set of features, including application management, security policy enforcement, and endpoint analytics. It provides a more comprehensive approach to managing all types of endpoints from a single console.

Advanced Persistent Threat (APT)

It refers to a sophisticated, long-term cyberattack carried out by skilled adversaries where the threat is both advanced as well as persistent. APT actors often target specific organizations or entities for espionage, data theft, or sabotage. They use various techniques, including social engineering, zero-day exploits, and custom malware.

Identity and Access Management (IAM)

A system that centrally manages and govern user identities, credentials, even MFA and access rights across systems, applications, and resources. IAM can be leveraged to achieve Single Sign On (SSO)

Patch Management Systems

Software solutions that automate the process of deploying and managing software patches and updates to address security vulnerabilities and improve system security.

Cloud Security Posture Management (CSPM)

CSPM acts as a vigilant overseer for your cloud infrastructure, scanning it for best practices, settings, identity and access management policies, data encryption settings, network configurations, and more.

By providing real-time visibility into your cloud security posture, CSPM enables organizations to proactively identify and address security risks before attackers can exploit them. It helps ensure that cloud resources are configured securely, reducing the likelihood of data breaches, unauthorized access, and compliance violations.

Cloud Native Application Protection Platform (CNAPP)

CNAPP is like a CSPM but for your cloud-native applications. CNAPP includes features such as container security, runtime protection, vulnerability scanning, and compliance monitoring. It helps organizations secure their containerized workloads, detect, and respond to threats in real-time, and maintain compliance with regulatory requirements and industry standards.

It promotes a DevSecOps approach, where security is integrated early and continuously throughout the development and deployment process.

Cloud Workload Protection Platform (CWPP)

CWPP acts as a security platform monitoring and protecting digital assets, ensuring their security and integrity in a dynamic cloud environment. CWPP offers features such as workload visibility, threat detection, vulnerability management, and compliance monitoring. It continuously scans and assesses your cloud workloads for security risks, such as misconfigurations, vulnerabilities, and unauthorized access attempts.

User and Entity Behavioural Analytics (UEBA)

UEBA continuously observes activities such as login patterns, file access, data transfers, and application usage to establish a baseline of normal behaviour for each user and entity.

If a user deviates from normal behaviour such as accessing sensitive files they've never accessed before or attempts to log in from an unusual location, UEBA may flag this behaviour as suspicious and trigger an alert for further investigation.

By correlating diverse data points and identifying deviations from established patterns, UEBA helps organizations detect insider threats, compromised accounts, and other malicious activities that traditional security measures might miss. It provides valuable insights into potential security incidents, enabling proactive response and mitigation efforts.

Digital Forensics

Digital Forensics is like being a cyber detective, investigating digital evidence to uncover the truth behind cyber incidents and criminal activities.

Digital Forensics experts carefully collect, preserve, and analyse evidence such as log files, emails, documents, and network traffic. They use specialized tools and techniques to reconstruct events, identify perpetrators, and determine the extent of the damage.

Behavioural Biometrics

Behavioural biometrics a cutting-edge authentication technology that analyses the way individuals interact with devices and applications to verify their identity. It creates a unique digital fingerprint based on your behaviour patterns, such as how you type on a keyboard or swipe on a touchscreen.

Imagine if your computer could recognize you not just by your face or fingerprint, but by how you move the mouse or how you type your passwords.

For example, if you're logging into an online banking portal, behavioural biometrics can analyse factors like your typing speed, keystroke dynamics, mouse movements, and touchscreen gestures to determine if you're the legitimate account holder. If your behaviour matches the established profile, you're granted access; if not, additional authentication measures may be required.

Cross-Site Scripting (XSS)

XSS is a digital Trojan horse, where malicious code is injected into a web application to exploit vulnerabilities and compromise the web application. It's a type of security vulnerability commonly found in web applications that allows attackers to inject and execute malicious scripts in the context of a user's web browser.

With XSS, an attacker could sneakily insert harmful code into a website's comments section, which, when displayed by the website, could steal their login credentials, expose user data, execute unauthorized commands, or redirect them to malicious websites.

Exploit Kit

An exploit kit is a tool used by cyber attackers to deliver malware onto target systems. It typically consists of a collection of malicious code, including exploits for various software vulnerabilities.

Exploit kits are often hosted on compromised websites or distributed through malicious emails. When a user visits a compromised website or clicks on a malicious link, the exploit kit scans the system for vulnerabilities and delivers the appropriate exploit to compromise it.

Cyber Range

Cyber Range is a virtual training ground for cybersecurity professionals, providing a realistic environment to practice and hone their skills in defending against cyber-attacks. The simulation environment replicates real-world networks, systems, and applications, allowing individuals and teams to simulate cyber-attack scenarios and fine-tune their incident response capabilities.

In a Cyber Range scenario, participants may be tasked with defending a simulated network from various cyber threats, such as malware infections, phishing attacks, or denial-of-service (DoS) attacks. The goal is to detect, respond and mitigate the attack using a plethora of security tools, implementing security best practices, while encouraging collaboration with team members.

Chapter 18

Epilogue: Securing the Future

As we conclude our journey through the dynamic realm of cybersecurity, let us reflect on the invaluable insights and strategies gleaned from "Cyber Resilience: A Strategic Handbook for Business Leaders." In today's interconnected world, the digital landscape is fraught with risks and challenges, but armed with knowledge and proactive measures, we can navigate these challenges with confidence and resilience.

Throughout this handbook, we have emphasized the importance of fostering a cyber-aware culture, driving continuous improvement, and embracing proactive risk management practices. By prioritizing cybersecurity as a strategic imperative and empowering employee at all levels to recognize and respond to cyber threats, organizations can enhance their resilience and safeguard their digital assets effectively.

As business leaders, it is our responsibility to champion cybersecurity initiatives, drive collaboration across departments, and stay vigilant against emerging threats. By remaining adaptable, proactive, and committed to ongoing learning and improvement, we can secure our organizations' digital future and protect the trust and confidence of our stakeholders.

In closing, let us remember that cybersecurity is not just a technology issue – it is a business enabler that requires leadership, collaboration, and a collective commitment to resilience. Together, let us embark on this journey with determination, courage, and a shared vision of securing a safer and more resilient digital future for all.

Rohit Srivastwa   Aalok Karnik

@rohit11      @aalok_the_k

/rohit11      /aalok